simple stories from the life of Jesus

ear and Simple Media
m Castor, editor

CLEAR & SIMPLE
——— M E D I A ———

Clear and Simple Media
linguistically simple, theologically clear, biblically faithful

ISBN 979-8-9909093-0-4

Permission requests can be sent via the CONTACT page at www.clearandsimplemedia.org.

Scripture passages in this book are based on four Bible translations that are designed with an ESL reader in mind.

New International Readers Version (NIrV)
Copyright© 1995, 1998, 2014 by Biblica, Inc.

Easy-to-Read Version (ERV)
Copyright© 2006 by Bible League International

EasyEnglish Bible (EEB)
Copyright© 2016 by MissionAssist, Worcestershire, UK

New Life Version (NLV)
Copyright© 1969 by 2003 Barbour Publishing, Inc.

Plain English Version (PEV)
Copyright© 2021 by Wycliffe Bible Translators, Inc.

Contents

Preface

This book is filled with stories about Jesus. None of the stories are long. But all of the stories will help you know who Jesus is and what he said.

We hope that you will enjoy the stories. We also hope that God will help you understand the stories. We hope that, in these stories, you will see that Jesus is the only one who can fix broken worlds and broken people.

But before you begin, there are some things you should know about how we wrote the book. We want the book to be clear and easy to read. That is why we wrote the book using a very simple set of words. In fact, we use a word list of only 2000 of the most common English words to tell all of the stories. **We wrote them for people who are new to the English language. And we wrote the stories for people who are new readers of the Bible.**

But there are some words in the book that may not be familiar to our readers. So, near the end of the book, you will find a Word List. Any word in this book with an * beside it is found in that list. Beside each word on the **Word List** is a definition of the word. The Word List will tell you what each of the words mean. Sometimes a word will have more than one meaning. This list will include the meanings that will help you best understand what you read.

Simple Stories from the Life of Jesus

Jesus is the most wonderful man who ever lived. If you do not know about Jesus, these stories will help you. And if you do know something about Jesus, these stories will remind you just how wonderful he is.

Other men have been prophets*. They spoke for God. But Jesus was God who spoke to men.

Other men were great kings. But Jesus is the greatest king. And his kingdom* will never end.

Other men lived good lives. But Jesus lived a life that was not just good. He lived a perfect life. Jesus always did the right thing. He always spoke the right words. He did everything that God, his Father, asked him to do.

Other men were wise. They understood many things and spoke in ways that helped many people. But Jesus was the wisest man of all. He taught people wonderful things. He talked about things that are important in this life and in the life to come.

The stories on these pages are all about Jesus. Each of the stories comes from the books of four men: Matthew, Mark, Luke, and John. Two of these men traveled with Jesus. The other two were close friends of men who knew him well. All of these men wrote their stories for the same reason. They wanted people to know who Jesus was. So, they talked about the surprising things that Jesus did. They told of the wise words that he spoke. They wrote about the kind of man he was. They had come to believe that Jesus was a man sent by God. In fact, they believed that Jesus was God who became a man. He was the one who created* all things. Now he had come to live among the people whom he had made.

Why did they tell these stories? They wrote these things so that other people would believe in Jesus too. And that was important for them because they knew something else about Jesus. They knew that everyone who believed in Jesus would have a new life. And that life would last for ever.

So, read these stories. Read them so well that, when you finish, you could tell them yourself. As you read, ask yourself what Matthew or Mark or Luke or John wanted you to know about Jesus. When you do, perhaps the same thing will happen to you that happened to them. You will see who Jesus is. And you will come to believe in him too.

How this book is put together

This book has sixty (60) stories from the life of Jesus. The stories come from all four of the Gospel* books from the New Testament*: Matthew, Mark, Luke, and John. Some of the stories come from only one of these books. Others of the stories can be found in more than one of these Gospel books. A few of the stories can be found in all four of the books. If we counted every story the Gospels tell about Jesus, there would be more than two hundred (200) stories. We have chosen sixty (60). When more than one Gospel writer tells the story, we try to put them together as best we can.

As you read, you will notice that each Gospel book tells Jesus' story from a different point of view. The writers all tell what they saw and heard Jesus say and do. Or they tell Jesus' story from what they learned from his closest followers*. But each writer tells those stories in a different way. Because that is an important thing to know, we have included a short introduction to each of the Gospel books. If you take time to read these pages, it will help you understand the stories in this book.

Sixty Stories

1. **John the Baptist**
   Luke 1:5–25, 57–80; 3:1–20

2. **The Angel and Mary**
   Luke 1:26–38

3. **The Angel Visits Joseph**
   Matthew 1:18–24

4. **Jesus Is Born**
   Luke 2:1–7

5. **The Shepherd's Visit**
   Luke 2:8–20

6. **Anna and Simeon**
   Luke 2:21–39

7. **The Wise Men**
   Matthew 2:1–12

8. **The Boy Jesus in the Temple**
   Luke 2:13–52

9. **The Baptism of Jesus**
   Matthew 3:13–17; Mark 1:9–11;
   Luke 3:21–22; John 1:29–34

10. **Jesus is Tempted**
    Matthew 4:1–11; Mark 1:12–13; Luke 4:1–13

11. **Jesus Changes Water to Wine**
    John 2:1–11

12. **Nicodemus**
    John 3:1–21

13. **The Woman at the Well**
    John 4:1–42

14. **The Men in Nazareth Deny Jesus**
    Luke 4:16–31

15. **Jesus Chooses His Disciples**
    Matthew 4:18–22; 9:9–13; Mark 1:16–20;
    2:13–17; 3:13–19; Luke 5:1–11, 27–32;
    6:12–16; John 1:40–51

16. **Jesus Heals a Man Who Cannot Walk**
    Matthew 9:1–8; Mark 2:1–12

17. **Jesus Heals a Man at the Pool**
    John 5:1–18

18. **The Sermon on the Mount**
    Matthew 5:1–7:29; Luke 6:20–45

19. **Build on the Rock**
    Matthew 7:24–27; Luke 6:46–49

Introduction to the Gospels

The word gospel* means a message or a notice of "good news." There are four books in the New Testament* called "the Gospels." Many people think that Mark* was the first of the Gospels. They think that Mark wrote it before Matthew*, John*, and Luke* wrote their books. Matthew and Luke may have read Mark's gospel and that helped them as they wrote their books. When Mark starts his book, he writes, "The beginning of the gospel of Jesus Christ." Soon the four books of Matthew, Mark, Luke, and John began to be known as 'the Gospels."

The Gospel According to Matthew*

There are many ways to start a book. Matthew* started his book with a list. On that list are the names of Jesus' family members. Matthew wanted you to know that Jesus could name his family all the way back to Abraham* and David*. Jesus was a son of Abraham, so he could be part of God's promise to Abraham. Jesus was a son of David, so he could be part of the promise that God made to David too. This was important to Matthew. Because Matthew wrote his book to tell us that Jesus was God's promised Savior*. He was the one who would keep the promise God made to Abraham. He was the king that God promised to David. The people called this promised Savior, the Messiah*. Messiah means "the One God has chosen." The word 'Christ' in the Greek language is the same as Messiah in the Hebrew language. Matthew wrote his book to help people see that Jesus was the Messiah. He was the one that the people of God had been waiting for for so long. Matthew wanted people to know this. That is why he talks so much in his book about the kingdom of God.

The Gospel According to Mark*

Most people think that Mark* wrote his book before Matthew, Luke, and John wrote their books. Mark was the first of the gospels. The book of Mark is also the shortest of the four gospels. Each of the gospels tells the same story. But each tells it in a different way. Mark talked about Jesus in many different ways in his book. He spoke of Jesus as God's most loved son. He spoke of him as the Son of Man. That was a title that Jesus often used for himself. Mark wanted to make sure that we know that. Mark told many of the same stories that the other gospels tell. But he left out many of the things that are in the other gospels.

Mark was a friend of Simon Peter.* Peter was one of the men that Jesus chose to follow him. Mark saw Jesus do many of the things that he writes about. And he also listened to Peter as he told him about what Jesus said and did. Matthew wrote his book to help the Jews* know about Jesus. Mark wrote his book for everyone. The people who were not Jews, Mark called Gentiles*. He wrote the way that he did because he wanted all people from all parts of the world to believe in Jesus.

The Gospel According to Luke*

Luke* was a disciple* of Jesus. But he was not one of Jesus' apostles*. Luke was a friend of Paul*. He was also a friend of many of the men and women who followed Jesus. He was probably not a Jew*. He listened when they told stories about Jesus. He wrote many of their stories in this book. The key words in Luke are 'son of man.' He put those words in his book almost 80 times.

He wrote his book to tell a friend about Jesus. He put many of the things that Jesus said into his book. He wrote about some of the things that Jesus did. He went step-by-step through Jesus' life. He wanted his friend to know the truth about Jesus. He wanted him to follow Jesus too.

Luke put many of the parables* that Jesus told in his book. He put more of those parables in his book than Matthew or Mark did. Many of the stories tell how Jesus loved the poor. He showed how Jesus cared about people whom other people did not care about.

Luke* was a doctor. He traveled with Paul on many of Paul's trips. Luke also wrote the book of Acts. He told about many of his trips with Paul in that book. Like Matthew and Mark, Luke wanted people to know Jesus and follow him for ever.

The Gospel According to John*

The last of the books called 'Gospels*' is John*. John was one of the men that Jesus chose and a close friend of Jesus. He wrote stories about Jesus, just as Matthew and Mark did. But John wrote the way that he did for a special reason. He wrote so that people would 'believe that Jesus is the Christ*, the Son of God.'

John called Jesus the 'Word.' He said that Jesus was with God before he created* the world. In fact, it was Jesus who made all things. Nothing was created that Jesus did not create. Jesus was God coming to us in a body. He showed people God's grace* and truth by living among them. When people saw Jesus, John said that they got to see God's glory*.

John builds his book around many of the miracles* that Jesus did among the people. Jesus healed a man who could not walk. He fed 5000 people with only a few fish and some bread. Jesus walked on the sea. John wrote about these miracles so that people would see who Jesus really is. John wanted the people to 'believe,' to trust* Jesus so that they could have eternal* life.

Introduction

Two thousand years ago, there was a group of people who lived in the Middle East. These people lived in a land that their fathers had lived in for many years. But they were not the only ones living in this land. A great army whose leaders lived in Rome*, a country far from them, were living in the land with them. This army was there to make certain that the people in that land followed the laws that the leaders in Rome gave them. When the people in Israel* made money from their work, they had to give part of that money to the leaders in Rome. They had to follow their rules. They had to pay them a tax. They could not choose their own leaders. The king in Rome made those decisions for them. And if the people did not obey these rules, the men in the army would put them in prison. Or, the army would take their land from them. Sometimes, they would even take their lives from them. The people did not like this, but there was not much they could do about it. They did not have their own army. And they did not have a king to lead them. But they did have hope*.

For more than a thousand years, prophets* had said that God would send someone to save them. They said that a son from Abraham's* family would come. That son would bless the whole earth. They said that a prophet like Moses* would come and lead the people. The prophets also reminded the people of the promise God had made to David*. He would have a son that would be a great king. His kingdom* would cover the whole world. And that kingdom would last for ever.

When the people talked to each other about this one who the prophets spoke about, they called this leader, "the Messiah*." That Messiah would come and when he came, he would put things right. He would give them what they had waited so long for. Freedom. He would fix the things that were broken and bring them peace*.

But it had been many years since God had sent a prophet to speak to them. And so they waited for this Messiah, this promised Savior* to come.

But then, something happened. God sent an angel* with messages for two people. The first message was for a priest named Zechariah*. The second message was for a young woman named Mary*.

It is with those two visits from the angel, and those two people, that this set of stories begins.

Jesus' Birth and Early Years

John the Baptist*

Luke 1:5-25, 57-80; 3:1-20

More than 2000 years ago, a man named Herod* was the king of Judea*. In those days, God's Temple* was in the city of Jerusalem*.

There was a priest* in the Temple in those days named Zechariah*. Zechariah's wife was Elizabeth*. They were both very old. Zechariah and Elizabeth loved God very much. And they obeyed God. But Elizabeth could not have children. So they had no sons or daughters.

One day, Zechariah went to the Temple. It was his time to serve in the Temple and make an offering* to God. As Zechariah did his work, an angel* of the Lord* went to Zechariah. And Zechariah was surprised. Then the angel said, "Do not be afraid. God hears your prayers. Elizabeth will have a son. You must name him John*. He will show many people in Israel* the way to God. He will speak like the prophet* Elijah*. And he will prepare the way for the Lord."

But Zechariah said, "Are you sure? My wife is old. So am I. How can this be?" The angel said, "My name is Gabriel*. I stand before God. You should have believed my words. But you did not. So, you will not be able to speak until after John is born. Everything I have said will happen, as God has chosen." Then Zechariah left the Temple. And he could not speak.

Not long after this, Elizabeth discovered that she was going to have a baby. When it was time for her to have her son, everyone was very happy for Elizabeth. The people asked Zechariah, "What will you name him?" But Zechariah still could not speak. Then Zechariah found something to write with. And he wrote, "His name is John." As soon as he did, Zechariah could speak again. Then, Zechariah began to praise* God and sing.

'Praise our Lord, the God of Israel. He promised long ago to save* us from those who hate us. Now he will keep that promise. And you, my child, will be a prophet of the Most High* God. You will go in front of the Lord and prepare the way for him. Your words will lead us to the way that brings peace*."

2

The Angel* and Mary*

Luke 1:26–38

After the angel* Gabriel* spoke to Zechariah*, God sent him to Nazareth*. Gabriel went there to speak to a young woman. Her name was Mary*. And she had never been with a man. She was a virgin*. But she had promised to marry a man named Joseph*.

So Gabriel went to Mary and said, "Hello, Mary. God loves you very much." But Mary was afraid when she saw the angel. And she did not understand why Gabriel had come. Then Gabriel said, "Do not be afraid. God has been kind to you. You will have a baby boy. And you will name him Jesus. He will be very great. And he will be the king of all of God's creation* for ever." Mary was amazed* by this. But she believed God's words.

Mary asked, "How will this happen? I have never been with a man." Gabriel said, "The Holy Spirit* will come to you. And the power of God Most High will make it so. The baby he gives you will be completely good. He will be called God's Son." Then Gabriel said, "There is more. Your cousin Elizabeth* is very old. And people said she could not have a baby. But God will give Zechariah and Elizabeth a son. And her baby will be born soon. All this is because there is nothing that God cannot do.'

When Mary heard this, she said, 'I am the servant of the Lord*. I know your words are true. Let all that you have said happen to me.' Then Gabriel left. And Mary did just as the angel had told her.

3

The Angel* Visits Joseph*

Matthew 1:18-24

Now Mary* had promised to marry a man named Joseph*. But before they were married, Joseph found out that Mary was to have a baby. Mary knew this baby was a gift from God. But Joseph did not know this yet. He was a good man. But he did not know what to do. He thought that he should leave Mary in secret. But he was very worried for Mary. "What should I do?" he thought. "This will bring shame upon us and upon our family." But as Joseph thought about what he should do, an angel* of God came to him in a dream*.

The angel said, "Joseph, you are a son of David*. You should take Mary to be your wife. But do not be afraid of what I am about to tell you. The baby Mary will have is a gift from God's Spirit*. And the baby will be a boy. You should name him Jesus. Because he will save* people from the wrong things they have done." God had spoken these things to a prophet* who lived a long time before Joseph. The prophet said a woman who had never been with a man would have a baby. And that people would call the baby, Immanuel*. This special name means "God with us." So Joseph knew the angel's words were true.

Then Joseph woke up from his dream. He did everything the angel said. And Joseph took Mary to be his wife. But he did not sleep with her as a man does with his wife until after the baby was born.

4

Jesus is Born
Luke 2:1-7

At the time when Mary* was to have her baby, Caesar Augustus* was king of the Roman* world. And he made a new law. Caesar Augustus said to his men, "I want to know how many people are in my kingdom*. Count every one of them." This was the first time that any king had counted the people in the Roman kingdom. So everyone had to go to his hometown to be counted.

Now Joseph* and Mary lived in a town called Nazareth*, in Galilee*. Joseph belonged to the family of King David. And King David had been born in Bethlehem*. So Joseph had to go to Bethlehem because Bethlehem was his hometown.

Joseph took Mary with him to Bethlehem. But when they got there, they could not find a good place to stay. And Mary was about to have her baby. So they had to sleep in the place where the animals ate their food. While they were in Bethlehem, Jesus was born. This was Mary's first baby. And the baby was a boy. It all happened like the angel* Gabriel* had told Mary. She wrapped the baby in cloth. And she laid the baby in an animal's feeding box.

5

The Shepherds* Visit

Luke 2:8-20

After Mary*'s baby boy was born, there were some shepherds* in a nearby field. The shepherds stayed with their sheep in the night. Then an angel* of the Lord* appeared to them. The sky filled with light. And God's glory* shone around them. The shepherds were very afraid. But the angel said, "Do not be afraid! Listen! I bring you good news. This news will make you very happy. Today in the town of David*, a baby was born. He is the one who will save* you. He is the one God said would come. He is the Messiah*, the Lord. You should go find this baby. His mother has wrapped him in cloths and laid him in an animal's feeding box."

Just then, many other angels filled the sky. And the sky shone very bright. The angels sang and praised* God with great joy. They sang, "God is great! He lives in the highest place. He has brought peace* to his people." Then the angels left the sky. The shepherds were amazed*. They said to each other, "This is very good news. We should go to Bethlehem*! We must find this baby that the angels have told us about."

So the shepherds went in a hurry to find the baby. They went to Bethlehem like the angel said. They found Mary, Joseph*, and the baby. The baby was wrapped in cloths. He was laying in the place where animals ate their food. The shepherds told Mary and Joseph about the angels. And the shepherds praised God. They were very happy.

When the shepherds left, they told everyone about the baby. What the shepherds said surprised everyone who heard it. But Mary remembered the shepherds' words. And she thought about their words for a very long time.

6

Anna* and Simeon*
Luke 2:21-39

When Jesus was eight days old, it was time for him to be circumcised*. This was a sign that the boy was part of the promise God made to Abraham*. And Mary* and Joseph* named the baby Jesus, just as the angel* Gabriel* had told them to do.

Soon, the time came for them to take Jesus to Jerusalem* to present him to God. The Scriptures* said, "The first male baby born to a woman belongs to me. So bring him to me. And you must also bring two birds for the priest* to kill. They will be a sacrifice*, an offering* to God." Mary and Joseph took Jesus to Jerusalem because they wanted to make that offering.

In those days, a man named Simeon* lived in Jerusalem. He loved and obeyed God's words. And the Holy Spirit* was with him. Simeon waited for a long time to see God bring comfort to Israel*. So the Holy Spirit told Simeon, "You will not die yet. You know God keeps his promises. And God has promised to send someone to save* Israel. And you will see God's Messiah* before you die."

One day, Simeon went to the Temple*. God's Spirit had told him to go there. And when he saw Jesus there, with Mary and Joseph, Simeon was very happy. He took Jesus and held him in his arms. And Simeon praised God and said, "Master, I am your servant. You have done what you promised. Now I know you will save your people." Mary and Joseph were surprised by what Simeon had said.

There was also a woman at the Temple, a widow named Anna*. She was very old. But she stayed at the Temple every day to pray and worship* God. When she saw Jesus, she gave thanks to God. Anna talked about Jesus to many people that day. And they spoke about the day that God would make Jerusalem free.

The Wise Men
Matthew 2:1-12

Before Joseph* and Mary* returned home to Nazareth*, they stayed in the city of Bethlehem*, in the country of Judea*. This was when Herod* was the king of Judea. After Jesus was born, wise men from the east came to Jerusalem*. They had come to Judea to look for someone. They asked, "Where is the child who is born the king of the Jews*? We saw his star in the sky. We came to worship* him." Herod heard about these men. And the wise men's questions made him very angry. The people in Jerusalem were worried, too.

So Herod met with some of the priests* who taught God's law*. Herod asked them where the king of the Jews was supposed to be born. They told Herod, "He will be born in Bethlehem in Judea. The prophet* Micah* wrote about him. Micah wrote about how God's ruler would come from Bethlehem. Micah said God's ruler would be like a shepherd* to his people." After that, Herod brought the wise men to him. But he did not want other people to know about it. He asked the wise men about the star. "You have to go to Bethlehem," he said. "But come back when you find the child. And tell me where he is. I want to worship him, too."

After this, the wise men left to find Jesus. They saw the star in the sky again. They followed it until it stopped over the house where Jesus and his mother Mary were. They were so happy. They went into the house and bowed down and worshiped Jesus. And they gave him gifts of gold, frankincense* and myrrh*. But after this, they had a dream*. In the dream, God told them: "Do not go back to Herod. He does not want to worship Jesus." When the dream was finished, they obeyed God. They returned home and did not return to Herod.

8

The Boy Jesus in the Temple*
Luke 2:13–52

After the wise men left, Joseph* had another dream*. God told Joseph that Herod* was angry. He wanted to find Jesus and hurt him. So Joseph must take his family and go to Egypt*. There, the boy would be safe. So Joseph did as he was told. He took his family to Egypt. But after some time passed, Herod died. Now it was safe for Joseph to return home. And so he did. He took Mary* and Jesus to Nazareth* to live. Jesus grew and learned many things. And even as a boy, he loved God's words.

Every year, Mary and Joseph went to Jerusalem* for a feast called Passover*. During the Passover, the people ate a special meal. They did it to remember when God had brought the people out of Egypt.

When Jesus was 12 years old, Mary and Joseph took Jesus to Jerusalem for the Passover. After the Passover time ended, Mary and Joseph left Jerusalem to go home. But Jesus stayed in Jerusalem. And Mary and Joseph did not know it. After they had traveled for one day, they looked for Jesus. They could not find him. So they went back to Jerusalem. They were very worried. And after three days, they found Jesus in the Temple*. Jesus was sitting, listening to the teachers there. And Jesus asked them questions. The teachers were surprised by how many things that Jesus understood.

But when Mary saw Jesus, she said, "My son, why are you here? We looked everywhere for you. But we could not find you. We were very troubled." But Jesus said to Mary, "You should have known that I would be in my Father's house. This is what I was born to do." But Mary and Joseph did not understand Jesus' words. So Jesus left Jerusalem with Mary and Joseph. But Mary remembered this. And she thought about what Jesus meant. But she did not yet understand.

In the days that followed, Jesus grew and became strong. He became more and more wise. And God's blessing* was upon him.

Jesus Begins His Public Life

9

The Baptism* of Jesus
Matthew 3:13-17; Mark 1:9-11; Luke 3:21-22; John 1:29-34

When Zechariah's* son, John*, had grown to be a man, he taught God's message near the Jordan River*. John said, "You have done many wrong things. Repent*! Change how you live. Ask God to forgive* you. And I will baptize* you." And John baptized many people who believed what he told them.

But when they saw John, some people thought that John might be the Messiah*. When John heard them, he said, "I baptize you with water. But someone else will come. And he will baptize you with the Holy Spirit* and with fire." But the people did not yet understand who John was speaking about.

Now Jesus had also grown to be a young man. One day, Jesus came to the Jordan River where John was. When John saw Jesus walk by, he said: "Look! It is God's chosen one! Jesus is the Lamb of God* and will take away the world's sins*!" Many people heard John. But they did not understand his words.

Then Jesus came to John and said, "John! I want you to baptize me." This surprised John. He even tried to stop Jesus. "No!" John said. "I need you to baptize me." But Jesus said, "This is the right thing for us to do." So, because John wanted to obey God, John baptized Jesus.

When Jesus came up out of the water, the skies opened up. And God's Spirit came down upon Jesus in a body that looked like a dove. Then a voice spoke from the heavens. "This is my Son. My chosen one. I am pleased with him." The skies closed, and the dove was gone. The people who saw this were amazed*. They had heard what John had said. And now they had heard God say that Jesus was his son. John saw the dove and heard the voice. Then he spoke to the people as a witness to what he had seen and heard. This Jesus, he told them, is the Son of God*.

Jesus is Tempted

Matthew 4:1–11; Mark 1:12–13; Luke 4:1–13

After John* baptized* Jesus, Jesus left the Jordan River*. And the Holy Spirit* led Jesus into the wilderness. While Jesus was there, Satan* tested Jesus. He tried to make Jesus disobey* God. This lasted for 40 days and 40 nights. And Jesus did not eat anything.

After 40 days, Jesus was very hungry. Satan knew that Jesus would be weak because he was so hungry. So Satan went to Jesus and said, "Are you really God's Son? If you are, tell these rocks to turn into bread." Jesus said, "No! The Scriptures* say that people do not live just by eating bread. They live by every word that comes from the mouth of God."

Then Satan took Jesus to Jerusalem*. They stood on the top of the Temple*. Satan said, "You say you are God's Son. So jump down from here." "After all," he said, "Didn't God say that the angels* will keep you safe?" But Jesus said, "No! The Scriptures say, 'Do not do a foolish thing to see if God will save* you. Do not put God to the test.'"

Finally, he took Jesus to a tall mountain. He showed Jesus all of the nations in the world. Then Satan said, "You can rule all these countries. You just have to bow to me. Worship* me, and I will give you everything we see from here." But Jesus answered him and said, "Leave me, Satan! The Scriptures say to worship God alone and serve only him." As soon as Jesus said this, Satan left him. Then God sent angels to take care of Jesus.

11

Jesus Changes Water to Wine
John 2:1–11

One day, Jesus' mother went to a wedding. The family invited Jesus and his disciples* to come too. The wedding was in the town called Cana*, in Galilee*. When the people at the party drank all the wine, there was nothing left. So Mary* went to Jesus. She told Jesus there was no more wine. But Jesus said, "Why do you tell me this? It is not yet time for me to do this." But Mary told the servants at the wedding to listen to Jesus. She told them to do whatever Jesus told them.

There were six big jars there. The jars were for water that the Jews* used to wash themselves for worship*. So Jesus told the servants to fill the pots with water. And the servants did just as Jesus told them. Then Jesus said, "Now take some water from the pots and give it to the master of the party." So the servants did what Jesus said. When the master of the party tasted it, he was very surprised. The water had become wine. And the wine tasted very good.

The master of the party called to the man who had just been married. He said, "At most weddings, they serve the best wine first. But you have saved the best wine until last!" He did not know where the wine came from. But only the servants knew it came from Jesus.

This was the first miracle* that Jesus did at Cana. This miracle helped people see Jesus' glory* - that Jesus was more than a man. When his disciples saw it, they believed in him.

Nicodemus*

John 3:1–21

There was a Pharisee* named Nicodemus*. The Pharisees were men who studied the Scriptures*. They followed the laws* of Moses* with great care. Nicodemus had heard many surprising things about Jesus. So Nicodemus came to speak to Jesus at night. He said to Jesus, "Teacher, we know that God sent you to us. You have done many amazing things."

Jesus replied, "What I tell you is true. Unless a man is born from above, he will not see God's kingdom*." But Nicodemus did not understand. So he asked, "How can a man be born when he is already old?" So Jesus said, "My words are true. You must be born of water and of God's Spirit* to enter God's kingdom. You remember when I said, 'You must be born from above.' The flesh gives birth to the flesh. The Spirit gives birth to the spirit."

Nicodemus asked, "How can this happen?" Jesus said, "You are an important Jewish* leader. Why do you not understand? You have heard my words. But you do not believe me. The Son of Man* came down from heaven*. And he will be lifted up. And everyone who trusts* him will live for ever with God. God loved the world so much that he sent his Son. So everyone who believes in the Son will not die. Instead, they will live for ever with God."

"God did not send his Son into the world to punish people. He came to save* them. So everyone who trusts in God's Son will be saved. Some people refuse to believe in God's one and only Son. Those people will be punished. Light has come into the world. But some people love the darkness more than the light. They love darkness because they do what is evil*. But whoever does what is true comes to the light."

13

The Woman at the Well

John 4:1-42

When Jesus left Nicodemus*, he went into the countryside. And many people followed Jesus and listened to him teach. On his way to Galilee*, Jesus stopped in Samaria*. Jesus and his disciples* had traveled for a long time. So Jesus' disciples left to go to the town to buy food. And Jesus sat down by the well called Jacob's well.

A woman from Samaria* came to the well to get some water. Jesus said to her, "Please, could you give me a drink." This surprised the woman. Because Jews* did not talk to people from Samaria. The woman replied, "You are a Jew, and I am from Samaria. Why would you ask me to give you a drink?" Jesus said, "You do not know who I am. If you did, you would have asked me to give you a drink. The water I have gives new life." The woman said, "Sir, where will you get this water that gives life?" Jesus answered, "Everyone who drinks from this well will be thirsty again. But the water that I give will never stop its flow. My well leads to life with God for ever."

This surprised the woman even more. "Sir," she said. "Give this water to me. Then I will never be thirsty again." So Jesus said, "Go and bring your husband." But the woman said, "I have no husband." Jesus said, "What you say is true. You have had five husbands. And the man you live with now is not your husband." Then the woman said, "Sir, I can see that you are a prophet* from God." Then she said, "I know the Messiah* will come. When he comes, he will tell us everything." Jesus answered, "The one you are talking about is the one who is speaking to you. I am he." The woman did not know what to say. So she left Jesus at the well. She went to her village. And she told everyone what Jesus had said. She told them that Jesus knew everything about her. Then, a large crowd came to Jesus. He taught them for two days. And many of the Samaritans believed in Jesus.

Jesus Teaches in Galilee*

14

The Men in Nazareth* Deny Jesus

Luke 4:16–31

By this time, many people followed Jesus. And he had taught them many things. After many days, Jesus decided to return to Nazareth*. Nazareth was Jesus' home. On the Jewish* day of rest, Jesus went to the place where the Jews* worshiped* called a synagogue*. The Jews went there to worship God and learn from the Scriptures*. When he got there, Jesus took a scroll* that recorded the words of Isaiah* the prophet*. He stood up and he began to read.

"The Spirit* of the Lord* God is on me. He has chosen me to tell God's good news to the people. He has sent me to tell people in prison, 'Go free!' I will say to people who cannot see, 'See again!' I must tell the people who are like slaves to be free. I must tell everyone, 'This is the year that God will be kind to his people.'" Then Jesus closed the book. And Jesus sat down. Then Jesus said, "These words have become true today."

But the people still did not understand. They said to each other, "This is Joseph*'s son. Is that not true?" But Jesus heard them. And Jesus said, "You do not believe what I have said. It is true that people do not accept God's prophet in his own town. When Elijah* was alive, the people did not believe his words. And when Elisha* was alive, the people did not believe his words." This made the people very angry. They made Jesus leave Nazareth. They were so angry that some of them wanted to kill Jesus. But Jesus left them. And they did not hurt him.

Jesus Chooses His Disciples*

Matthew 4:18-22; 9:9-13; Mark 1:16-20; 2:13-17; 3:13-19;
Luke 5:1-11, 27-32; 6:12-16; John 1:40-51

After Jesus came out of Nazareth*, he began to preach*. He told people to turn away from evil*. Then he told them about the kingdom* of God. And Jesus began to gather a group of men to join him.

One day, Jesus walked by the Sea of Galilee*. He saw two brothers, Simon Peter* and Andrew*. They were fishermen. "Come and follow me," Jesus said. "I will send you to fish for people." Simon Peter and Andrew left their nets and followed Jesus.

Then Jesus saw two other brothers, James* and John*. They were in a boat with their father. Jesus called out to them. They left their boat and their father and followed Jesus.

Later, Jesus saw a man named Matthew*. He collected taxes from people. Jesus said, "Come and follow me." So Matthew got up and followed him. Matthew invited Jesus into his house for dinner. There, many other tax collectors and sinners* ate with Jesus. The Pharisees* thought that Jesus should not eat with these people. Jesus heard the Pharisees say this. And Jesus said, "Healthy people do not need a doctor. Sick people do. I am not here for the people who think God is happy with them. I am here so that sinners will follow me." But the Pharisees did not understand Jesus.

Some time later, Jesus went up on a mountain. There, he prayed to God for a long time. After he had prayed, he called some of his followers* to come to him. He made 12 of them disciples*. He would later send them out to preach. There was Simon, who Jesus called Peter. There was James, the son of Zebedee, and John. There were Andrew*, Philip*, Bartholomew*, Matthew, Thomas* and James, the son of Alphaeus. And there were Jude* and Simon the Zealot*. Judas* Iscariot was also one of the 12. Judas Iscariot would later give Jesus to his enemies.

16

Jesus Heals a Man Who Cannot Walk

Matthew 9:1-8; Mark 2:1-12

After Jesus chose the men who would follow him, he returned to Capernaum*. Soon, people heard that he had come home. And a large crowd gathered to hear him. Four men came, and brought their friend to Jesus. The men carried him on a mat. Their friend could not walk. But when they got to the house, they could not get the man inside. There were too many people. So they went up to the roof. And they made a hole in the roof and lowered the man down to where Jesus was. Jesus saw that the men trusted* in him. So Jesus said to the man on the mat, "Do not be afraid. I forgive* you for all of the wrong things you have done. Your sins* are forgiven."

But some teachers of the law* of Moses* were angry at Jesus for his words. They said, "Jesus says things that no man should say. Only God can forgive sins." But Jesus knew their thoughts. So Jesus said to them, "Why do you think such bad things? Which is easier, to forgive this man's sins? Or to tell him to get up and walk when he cannot? But I want you to know this. The Son of Man* has the power on earth to forgive sins."

Then Jesus looked at the man on the mat. And Jesus said to him, "Get up. Pick up your mat, and go home." As soon as Jesus spoke, the man got up. The man picked up his mat and went home. Everyone saw him. And they were all surprised. And they praised* God and said, "God is great. We have never seen anything like this before."

17

Jesus Heals a Man at the Pool

John 5:1-18

One day, Jesus decided to go to Jerusalem*. It was time for one of the Jewish* festivals. There was a pool in Jerusalem called Bethesda*. Many sick people lay around the pool. The sick people waited for the water in the pool to move. They all believed that an angel* would come down to the pool and move the water. The first person to go into the pool would be made well. Many sick people had waited there for a long time.

There was a man who had come to the pool for 38 years. Jesus saw the man. And he knew that the man had been ill for a very long time. So Jesus asked the man, "Do you want to be well?" This man could not walk. So he answered Jesus, "Sir, I do not have anyone to help me into the pool. So I am never the first person into the pool." But Jesus said to him, "Get up! Pick up your mat and walk!" And immediately, the man picked up his mat and began to walk.

This happened on a Jewish day for rest - the Sabbath*. And when the Jewish leaders heard about the man who had been sick, they were angry with Jesus. So the Jewish leaders asked the man who had made him well. But he did not know.

Later, Jesus saw the man in the Temple*. Jesus said to him, "Look, you are well again. Now stop sinning or something worse may happen to you."

So the man returned to the Jewish leaders. And he told them that it was Jesus who had healed him. The Jewish leaders were very angry that Jesus had healed a man on the day of rest. But Jesus said to them, "My Father works. So I must work too." This made the Jewish leaders even more angry. Because Jesus said that God was his Father. He was saying that he was equal with God. And the Jewish leaders wanted to kill Jesus for this.

18

The Sermon on the Mount

Matthew 5:1-7:29; Luke 6:20-45

Now, many people began to follow Jesus. One day, Jesus saw a crowd had gathered. So he went up on a hill and sat down. Then he began to teach them and said, "Blessed* are the ones who know they are needy people. They will see God's kingdom*. Those who are hungry will be fed. And if your desire to please God is as strong as their hunger for food, you will be full. Blessed are you when people hate you because you follow me. A long time ago, people treated the prophets* the same way. But be glad. Because you will be blessed in heaven*."

Then Jesus told his disciples* what they should do. "Love your enemies. Give to everyone who asks you. And do not keep things for yourself. Do to others what you want them to do to you. Do not only be nice to people you like. Even sinners* can do that. But you should love your enemies. Do good to them. If you do this, you are children of God. For this is just what God does."

"Do not worry about your life. God sees you. He knows what you need. Put God's kingdom first. Do what he wants you to do. And he will give you what you need. And when you pray, do not stand on street corners so everyone can see you. Go into your house and pray in a secret place. The Father sees you. He knows what you need. And when you pray this way, your Father will reward you. This is how you should pray."

"Our Father in heaven. May all people respect your name. We pray that your kingdom will come. And all that you want to be done will be done on earth, the same as it is in heaven. Give us the bread we need today. And forgive* us when we do wrong, as we forgive those who do us wrong. Keep us from sin* when we are tempted. And save* us from the Evil One*."

19

Build on the Rock

Matthew 7:24-27; Luke 6:46-49

As Jesus taught the people from the hill, he said things about this life and the life to come. He told stories that the people would remember.

"Do any of you have a son? If he asks for bread, will you give him a stone? Even though you may be bad people, you know how to give good things to your children. So your Father in heaven* will give good things to those who ask.

"Ask, and what you ask for will be given to you. Seek, and you will find what you are looking for. Knock, and God will open the door."

Then, Jesus told a story about two men. Each man built a house. One man built his house on a rock. The other man built his house on the sand. "Then," Jesus said, "The sky became dark, and a storm came. The storm brought so much water that it became a flood. But the flood did not hurt the first house because the man had built it on a rock. That same storm came to the other man's house. The sky became dark, and the wind blew. When the flood came, water hit the house. And the house on the sand fell down."

Then Jesus told them what the story was to teach them. "Some people hear my words and obey them. These people are like the man who built his house on the rock. Other people hear my words but do not obey me. These people are like a man who built his house on the sand."

Some people listened and understood what Jesus said. Other people heard the same stories but did not understand them. But when Jesus was finished, all of the people were amazed* at Jesus' words. Jesus spoke with great power. His words were not like the words of the teachers they had known before.

20

The Roman* Officer's Servant

Matthew 8:5-13; Luke 7:1-10

When Jesus had finished speaking from the hill, he went into Capernaum*. A man in the Roman* army was there. He was an important man, an officer. He came to Jesus and told him a story about his servant. He liked his servant very much. But the servant was sick. The officer heard about Jesus. So he came to Jesus and said, "Lord*, my servant is very sick. I am afraid that he will die."

Jesus knew the man was worried. So Jesus said to the officer, "I will go to your house and heal your servant." The officer answered, "Lord, I am not good enough for you to come into my house. I know that if you only speak, my servant will be healed. I have men who work under me. I only need to say, 'Go', and they go. I say to another, Do this! And he does it."

When Jesus heard this, he was amazed*. Then Jesus turned to his followers*. He said, "This man trusts* me more than anyone I have met. Even more than anyone in Israel*." This surprised the crowds. They thought that only people from Israel could trust Jesus. But Jesus said, "People think just because they are Israelites* they can come into my kingdom*. But many people will come from the east and the west. They will sit and eat in God's kingdom. But many who do not trust in me will be thrown out into the darkness. "

Jesus looked at the officer. "Go home," Jesus said. "When you get there, you will see your servant. And he will be healed like you believed." The Roman officer went home and found that his servant was healed, just like Jesus had promised.

21

Jesus is Blessed*

Luke 7:36–50

One day, a Pharisee* asked Jesus to eat with him. So Jesus went to the Pharisee's house. A woman who had done many wrong things heard about this. And she went to the Pharisee's house to see Jesus. She took a small jar of oil to the house with her. The oil had a very nice smell. And it was worth a lot of money. When the woman saw Jesus, she bowed at his feet. And she cried. She wiped Jesus' feet with her hair. She kissed Jesus' feet and poured oil on them.

When the Pharisee saw this, he said, "This woman should stop. If Jesus were a prophet*, he would know what kind of wicked woman she is." But Jesus said to him, "I will tell you a story. There once were two men. They both had borrowed money from someone. One man borrowed 500 coins. The other man borrowed 50 coins. But neither man had enough money to pay back what they owed. So the man that had lent them the money said, 'I will forgive* what you owe me.'" Then Jesus asked the Pharisee, "Which man would love him the most?" And the Pharisee answered, "The man who needed to pay back the most money." Jesus said, "You are right."

Then Jesus looked at the woman. And he spoke to the Pharisee. "When I came into your house, you did not give me water to wash my feet. This woman has washed my feet with her tears. You did not give me a kiss to welcome me. But this woman has not stopped kissing my feet. I tell you that her many sins* are forgiven. That is why she has done what she has done. But the one who has been forgiven little, loves little."

Then Jesus said to the woman, "Your sins* are forgiven." This surprised the people who heard him. And they said, "Who is this man? How can he forgive sins?"

Then Jesus looked at the woman and said, "Your faith* has saved* you. Go in peace*."

22

Different Kinds of Soil
Matthew 13:1-23; Mark 4:3-8, 14-20; Luke 8:5-8, 11-15

Jesus traveled near the lake in Galilee* once again. He taught many people there. As he was teaching, he told them a story, a parable* about a farmer.

Jesus said to the crowd, "Listen to me! One day, a farmer went to his field to plant some seeds. He walked about the field and threw seeds onto the dirt. Some seeds fell onto the path. And some birds flew by as he scattered the seeds. And the birds ate the seeds from the path. Other seeds fell onto rocks where there was very little soil. These seeds began to grow, but there was not enough soil. And when they grew, the sun quickly burned the little plants. And the little plants died.

Other seeds fell into thorn bushes. The bushes grew when the little plants grew. The thorn bushes grew too big and the little plants could not grow. So the little plants died. But other seeds fell onto good soil. Those seeds grew. Soon, there were many big and healthy plants in the good soil. Those plants produced much fruit." But the people did not understand Jesus' story.

So Jesus said to his disciples*, "I will tell you what this means. The seeds are like God's words. The farmer is like someone who tells others about God's words. Some seeds fall on the path. And Satan* comes and takes them away so that some people won't believe. Some seeds fall among the rocks. They are like people who are happy to trust* God's words for a short time. Then trouble comes or people are not kind to them. So they stop and do not grow any more. Other seeds fall among thorn bushes. These are like the people who worry about this life. They are like the people who think only about the good things that they want to have. Because of those things, the word is crowded out. And there is no fruit from their lives.

But some seeds fall onto good soil. These seeds are like the people who hear God's words. They understand the words. They trust in God. They grow and their lives show much fruit."

The Treasure and the Pearl*

Matthew 13:44-46

Jesus taught the people many things. And common people followed him gladly. He spoke and lived to help people see what God is like. When he had told many stories, Jesus left the crowd. His disciples* came to him and he told them two stories about the kingdom* of heaven*.

Jesus said, "Listen to me! I will tell you what the kingdom of heaven is like. The kingdom of heaven is like something valuable that someone hid in a field. Another man found it and then he hid it again. And he was very happy because of what he found. Then that man sold everything he had and he bought that field."

"Again," Jesus said, "the kingdom of heaven is like this. A man had a business. And he looked for fine pearls to buy. One day, he found one that was beautiful and very valuable. So the man went home. And he sold everything he had. And he went and bought the pearl."

Not everyone understood Jesus' words. But some people did understand. They knew Jesus meant that the kingdom of heaven is worth everything. The kingdom of heaven is more valuable than all that you own.

24

Jesus Stops the Storm

Matthew 8:23-27; Mark 4:35-41; Luke 8:22-25

One day, Jesus came to the town of Capernaum*. He spent many days there telling stories to the crowds. Jesus healed many people too. They were by Lake Galilee*, so Jesus got into a boat. And he told his disciples*, "Let us go to the other side." So the disciples left the crowd and got into the boat. As they went, a great storm began to blow across the lake. Waves came over the sides of the boat. Water came into the boat. And the disciples were very afraid. They thought that they would die in the boat. Now Jesus was in the back of the boat. And he was asleep.

The disciples hurried to wake Jesus. They said, "Master, save* us! We will die here on the water!" So Jesus stood. He looked at the wind and the waves and said, "Be still!" Immediately, the wind stopped and the waves were quiet.

Then Jesus looked at his disciples. He said to them, "Why are you afraid? Do you still not trust* me?" When the men saw what Jesus did, they were afraid. They asked each other, "What kind of man is this? Even the wind and waves obey him!"

25

The Mad Man
Matthew 8:28-34; Mark 5:1-20; Luke 8:26-39

After the storm, Jesus and his disciples* went to the other side of Lake Galilee*. They arrived at the place where the Gadarene* people lived. When Jesus got out of the boat, he saw a man. This man lived in the caves where the villagers buried dead people. An evil spirit* lived in this man. And the man was very strong because of this. No one could keep him tied up. Many people in Gadara* had tried to put him in chains, but he always broke the chains. And he would cry out and cut himself with rocks.

When this man saw Jesus, he ran to him. Then he fell on his knees at Jesus' feet. Jesus spoke and said, "Evil spirit! Come out of this man!" But before Jesus finished, the man said in a loud voice, "What do you want with me? You are Jesus, Son of the holy* God. Please do not hurt me." Jesus asked the evil spirit, "What is your name?" The man said, "My name is Legion because we are many."

There was a large group of pigs on a hill near there. So the evil spirit said to Jesus, "Please just send us into the pigs." So Jesus said, "Go!" Immediately, the spirits left the man and went into the pigs. The pigs ran down the hill and into the lake. All of the pigs died. When this happened, the men who cared for the pigs were afraid. The people from the town came to see what had happened. They saw the man who had been filled with evil spirits. He sat at Jesus' feet. He wore clothes and he was healed. When the people saw this, they were afraid. So they came to Jesus and asked him to leave the village.

As Jesus got into the boat, the man who had been full of evil spirits came to him. He asked Jesus if he could go with him. But Jesus said, "No. Go home to your friends. Tell them how much the Lord* has done for you." And that is just what he did. When people heard his story, they were amazed*.

26

Jairus*'s Daughter

Matthew 9:18-26; Mark 5:21-24, 35-43; Luke 8:40-41, 49-56

When Jesus and the disciples returned to Capernaum*, they met a large crowd. Jesus began to teach the people. And a Jewish* leader came to Jesus. His name was Jairus*. He fell to his knees in front of Jesus. Jairus said, "Jesus! My daughter will die very soon. But if you come with me, you can make her better. Then my daughter will live." So Jesus went with him. Jesus' disciples* went with them too.

When they were on the road, some men from Jairus' house came to them. "Sir," they said to Jairus. "Your daughter is dead. Jesus should not come. There is nothing he can do now." When Jesus heard the men, Jesus said, "Jairus, do not be afraid. Instead, trust* me."

When they came to Jairus' house, Jesus, Peter*, James*, and John* went into the house. All of Jesus' other disciples stayed outside. There was a crowd of people in the house. They cried very much. But Jesus said, "Do not be afraid. And you should not cry. The girl is not dead. She is only asleep." But the crowd laughed at Jesus. So Jesus made the crowd leave the house. Jairus and his wife stayed with Jesus. Then Jesus held the girl's hand. He said, "Talitha koum." This means, "Little girl, stand up." Immediately the little girl stood up. She began to walk. Then Jesus said to them, " Give the girl some food. And do not tell anyone what I have done." The little girl was twelve years old.

John* in Prison
Matthew 14:1–12; Mark 6:14–29

King Herod* heard about the many good works Jesus had done. Jesus had healed many sick people. And he had become well known.

One day, John* the Baptist went to Herod. John followed the law*. And he wanted others to follow the law. So John said to Herod, "You should not be married to your brother's wife, Herodias*. It is against the law of Moses." This made Herod angry. So Herod had John the Baptist arrested. But Herod was afraid of John. Herod knew the people thought John was a prophet*. He kept John safe because he liked to listen to him.

Herodias* wanted John to die. But Herod was too afraid. One day, Herod gave a special meal for his birthday. At the party, the daughter of Herodias danced for Herod and his guests. She pleased Herod very much. So he promised to give her anything she asked for. Herodias told her daughter, "Ask Herod to give you John's head." So the girl obeyed Herodias.

The girl said to Herod, "Give me John the Baptist's head on a plate." These words made Herod very sad. But it was too late. The people at Herod's party had heard him make the special promise to the girl. So Herod told his guards, "Go to the prison. And bring me the head of John the Baptist." So the guards obeyed Herod.

After this happened, John's followers went to the prison. They got John's body and buried it. They told Jesus. When Jesus heard this, he took a boat to a place where he could be alone.

Jesus Leaves Galilee*

28

Jesus Feeds the Five Thousand

Matthew 14:13-21; Mark 6:30-44; Luke 9:10-17; John 6:1-15

After John* the Baptist died, Jesus left the crowds to be alone. But the crowds followed him. There were many sick people in the crowd. And Jesus felt sorry for them. The people were like sheep without a shepherd*. So Jesus began to teach them many things. He healed many who were sick. And it was nearly time for the Jewish* Passover* Feast.

After a long time, Jesus' disciples* came to him. They said, "Jesus, it will be dark soon. Send the people away so they can find something to eat." But Jesus said, "Do not send the crowds away. Instead, give them something to eat." Jesus' disciples could not believe what Jesus said. "Lord*," they said. "How would we do that? To feed these people would take more money than what we have." There were 5,000 men, not including women and children.

Then Andrew* saw a little boy. The boy had five small loaves and two fish. So Andrew took the boy to Jesus. "Look, Lord," Andrew said. "There is a boy here with five small loaves and two fish." So the boy gave what he had to Jesus.

The disciples told the crowd to sit down. Then Jesus took the food. And he thanked God. Jesus broke the bread and fish into pieces. And the disciples gave the bread to the crowd. Everybody ate. They all ate until they were not hungry anymore. Then the disciples walked through the crowd. They collected all the food that had not been eaten. And they collected 12 baskets full of bread and fish. And all the people began to say, "This must be the prophet* who is to come into the world."

29

Jesus Walks on Water

Matthew 14:22-33; Mark 6:45-52; John 6:16-21

Immediately after Jesus fed the crowd, he told his disciples* to get back onto the boat to cross the lake. Then Jesus sent the crowd away. Then Jesus went up on a mountain to pray. And he prayed for a very long time. Soon, it became dark. Jesus' disciples were still in the boat on the lake.

Then a large storm came. The winds blew against them and the water was rough. And Jesus' disciples were trying very hard to control the boat. When it was nearly dawn, the winds still blew. And Jesus came toward his disciples, walking on the water . When the disciples saw this, they were very afraid. They did not know it was Jesus. Immediately Jesus said, "Do not be afraid! It is me." And Jesus came toward the boat.

But Simon Peter* said, "Lord*? Is it really you? If it is you, tell me to come to you on the water." So Jesus said, "Come to me." So Peter got out of the boat. And he began to walk toward Jesus. But Peter saw the strong wind. And he became very afraid. He began to sink. Simon Peter shouted, "Lord, save* me!" So Jesus took hold of Peter with his hand. And Jesus said to Peter, "Your faith* is so small. Why did you doubt?"

Then Jesus and Simon Peter got into the boat. And the wind immediately stopped. All the disciples praised Jesus and said, "It is true! You truly are God's Son!"

Transfiguration*
Matthew 17:1-13; Mark 9:2-13; Luke 9:28-36

Jesus continued to do many amazing things. And he told many stories to crowds of people.

A few days passed, and Jesus went up to a mountain to pray. He took Peter*, James*, and John* with him. As Jesus prayed, he began to change. He looked different. His face was bright like the sun. And his clothes became white. Then two men began to talk to Jesus. They were Moses* and Elijah*. Peter, James, and John were very afraid. They did not know what to do.

Then Peter said to Jesus, "Lord*, let me build three shelters. I will build one for you, one for Moses, and one for Elijah." But as Peter said this, a voice spoke from the clouds. It said, "This is my Son. I am pleased with him. Listen to him." And the disciples* were afraid. They fell to the ground. But Jesus came to them and put his hand on them. Jesus said, "Stand up. And do not be afraid." When the disciples looked up, they only saw Jesus.

Jesus left the mountain with Peter, James, and John. He said to them, "Do not tell anyone what happened. One day, the Son of Man* will die. And then he will become alive again. After these things happen, you can tell people what you saw on the mountain today." So the disciples did what Jesus said.

31

The Unkind Servant

Matthew 18:21-34

One day, Peter* came to talk to Jesus. Peter asked, "Lord*, if my friend does wrong things against me, how many times must I forgive* my friend? Should I forgive my friend seven times?" Jesus replied, "No, not seven times. You should forgive your friend 77 times!"

Then Jesus told Peter a story "The kingdom* of heaven* is like a king who wanted to collect all the money his servants owed him. The king found a servant who owed him 10,000 coins. But the man could not pay the king. So the king said, 'You must sell all that you have so that you can pay me.' But the servant fell on his knees. He said, 'Lord, please. Give me time. I promise to pay everything back.' So the king felt sorry for the man. The king forgave the man's debt and let him go.

Then that same servant went away and found another man who owed him 100 coins. He put his hands around his neck and said to him, 'Give me what you owe me.' He was very angry. The other man fell on his knees and said, 'Please, give me time. I will pay you back.' But the servant would not agree. And he had the man thrown in prison. Other people saw what the servant did, and they told the king. The king went to the servant. And he said, 'You are a very bad person. Did you forget the kindness I showed you? I forgave your debt. And you owed me much more than this man owes you.' And the king was very angry with the servant. So he threw him in prison. He would stay in prison until he paid what he owed the king."

Then Jesus said, "You must forgive your friends completely. If you do not forgive them, my Father in heaven will do what the king did. And he will not forgive the many wrong things you have done against him."

Jesus Teaches in Judea*

32

The Blind Man

John 9

One Sabbath* day, as he walked with his followers*, Jesus saw a blind man. This man had been blind since he was born. Jesus' disciples* asked, "Lord*, why is this man blind? Did his parents do wrong things, or did he?" Jesus answered, "No, it is not because this man or his parents did wrong things. But he is blind so that God could show his great work in this man." So Jesus walked up to the man. And Jesus spit in the dirt. He made mud with the dirt. And Jesus put the mud on the man's eyes. Then Jesus said, "Go and wash in the Siloam* pool." So the man did what Jesus said. Immediately, the man could see.

When he went home, his friends asked the man who healed him. So the man said, " A man they call Jesus put some mud on my eyes. When I washed it from my eyes, I could see." So the people brought the man to the Pharisees*. The man who had been blind told them what Jesus had done. Then some of the Pharisees said, "This man does not obey the laws about the Sabbath. He cannot be from God." But others of them said, "How can a man who is a sinner* do things like this?" So they asked again, " What do you have to say about this man?" Then the man said, "He is a prophet*!"

Then they sent for the man's parents. The parents told the Pharisees that their son had been blind. But they did not know that Jesus had healed him. So the Pharisees asked the man again. "Tell the truth," they said. "We know this man is a sinner." But the man said, "I do not know if he is a sinner or not. But this is what I do know. I was blind but now I can see." So the Pharisees sent the man away.

When Jesus heard about this, he went and found the man. Jesus asked him, "Do you believe in the Son of Man*?" The man answered, "Tell me who he is. Then I will believe in him." Jesus said, "He is the one who is speaking to you." Then the man believed and he began to worship* Jesus.

Good Samaritan*

Luke 10:25-37

One day, when Jesus was on his way to Jerusalem*, a Pharisee* came to him. He asked, "Teacher, what must I do to live with God for ever?" Jesus said, "What does God's law* say?" The Pharisee answered, "We must love the Lord* our God completely. We should love him the most. And we must love other people as much as we love ourselves." Jesus said, "This is true. If you do this, you will live with God forever." But the Pharisee wanted to test Jesus. So he asked, "Teacher, who are the people I must love? Who is my neighbor?" So Jesus told a story.

Jesus said, "A man walked down a path. But some men attacked him. They took away all his clothes and beat him. He was almost dead when they left. A priest* from the Temple* walked down the path. But when he saw the man, he did not stop. Then another priest, a Levite*, walked down the path. And he did not stop for the man. But then a man from Samaria* walked down the path. When he saw the man, he felt very sorry for him. And he gave him oil and wine and wrapped his wounds in clean cloths. Then he put the man on his donkey. He took him to a place where he could stay. And he took care of the man. The next day, the man from Samaria gave the man who managed the house two coins. And he paid for the man to stay there until he was better."

Then Jesus said, "Three men saw the man when he was hurt on the road. But which man was a neighbor to him?" The Pharisee answered, "The man who cared for him." And Jesus said, "Yes, so go and do as he did."

34

Mary* and Martha*
Luke 10:38-42

Jesus' disciples* followed him everywhere he went. One day, Jesus went to a village. There was a woman named Martha* who lived in the village. Martha called Jesus and his disciples to come to her home. So Jesus went. When he got there, he began to teach the people many things. Mary* was Martha's sister. Mary sat at Jesus' feet. And she listened carefully to Jesus' words. But Martha was busy doing all of the work for the many people in the house.

So Martha said to Jesus, "Lord*, my sister has left me alone to do all of the work. Tell her that she has to help me."

And Jesus, when he heard Martha's words said, "Martha, you are worried and troubled about many things. But only one thing is truly important. And Mary has chosen to do it. No one will take that away from her."

35

The Rich Fool

Luke 12:13-21

One day, a large crowd followed Jesus. Then someone in the crowd said to Jesus, "Teacher, my father has died. Tell my brother to give me my part of the things that our father left us." Jesus said, "It is not for me to judge between you and your brother."

Then Jesus looked at the crowd. He said, "Be careful! It is not good to want more things than you need. A person's life is worth more than what they have."

Then Jesus told them a story. "A man planted some seeds in good ground. The seeds began to grow. And they produced a lot of grain. The man thought about all of the crops that he would soon have. And he said, 'I have planted a lot of seeds. But where will I keep my crops?' But then he decided what to do. 'I know what I will do,' he said. 'I will pull down my old buildings. Then I will build a new and bigger building. I will keep my crops there.'"

"Then I will say to myself, 'You have lots of grain. You have enough stored away for many years. Now I can rest, eat and drink and enjoy an easy life."

"But then God said to the man, 'You are a fool. You will die tonight. Then who will have all that you have put away?'"

"This is how it will be for anyone who gathers things only for himself. He will have nothing if he is not rich in the ways of God."

Jesus Teaches from Beyond the Jordan*

Lost Sheep and Lost Coin

Matthew 18:12-14; Luke 15:4-10

Wherever he went, Jesus continued to heal sick people. And he continued to tell stories. Many people came to listen to him. Some were tax collectors. Others were people who lived in ways that did not please God. When the Pharisees* saw this, they said bad things about Jesus. "The man welcomes sinners* and eats with them," they said. Jesus heard them. So Jesus told them another story.

Jesus said, "A man had 100 sheep. But one day, he discovered that one of his sheep was not with the others. What does he do?" Jesus said, "The shepherd* leaves all of his other sheep on the hillside. And he goes to look for the one lost sheep. Listen to my words. When the shepherd finds the lost sheep, he is very happy. All the other sheep are safe together. But they do not make him as happy as the one sheep he found. And he returns home and tells all of his friends. The shepherd says, 'My friends, be happy with me. I have found my lost sheep!'"

Then Jesus said, "God, your Father in heaven*, is like the shepherd. He does not want any of his children to be lost. And there is great happiness in heaven when one who was lost is found. Yes, there is more happiness than for the 99 people who are already safe."

Then Jesus said, "A woman had ten coins. Then she lost one of them in her house. What do you think she will do? She will get a light and look everywhere in that house. She will keep on looking for her coin until she finds it. When she finds it, she will be happy. She will call out to her family, and to her friends. She will say, 'Look, I have found my lost coin. We can all be happy together now.'

In the same way, whenever somebody turns back to God, the angels* in heaven are very happy. Whenever one bad person stops doing bad things and turns to God, it makes God happy too."

37

The Lost Son

Luke 15:11-32

Then Jesus told another story. "There was a man with two sons. The younger son said, 'Father, give me now my part of the things I will get when you die.' So the father gave both sons a part of his things. And the younger son left their home. He went to a different country. And he was foolish. He spent all of the money that his father had given him. Soon the rain stopped. And there was no food anywhere. And the younger son was very hungry. So he went to a man in that country. And the man sent him to feed the pigs. The younger son was so hungry that he wanted to eat the pigs' food. But he had nothing to eat. Then the boy said to himself, 'Even my father's servants have plenty of food. I will go to my father's house. I will tell him that I am not good enough to be called his son. I will work as his servant.'

So the younger son went home. His father saw his son on the road. And he loved him. He ran to his son and kissed him. But the son said, 'Father, I have done many bad things. I should not be called your son.' But the father called his servants. And he told them to give the son a beautiful coat, a ring, and sandals for his feet. And the father told the servants to prepare a big meal. He wanted them to all be happy together.

When this happened, the older son was in the field. And when he heard what had happened, he was very angry. He said to his father, 'I work very hard for you. I have always done what you asked. But you never have a big meal for me. But this son who wasted everything has come home. And you are making a feast for him?" The father said, 'My son, you are always with me. Come be happy with us! We thought that your brother was dead. But he is alive. And now he has come home.'"

38

Lazarus*

John 11:1-44

One day, Jesus went with his disciples* across the Jordan River*. Many people from the villages near that place came to see him. Jesus taught them when they came. And many believed.

There was a man who lived in Bethany* named Lazarus*. He lived there with his sisters, Mary* and Martha*. Lazarus became ill. So Lazarus' sisters sent a message to Jesus. The message said, "Lord*, your friend is ill."

When Jesus heard this, he said, "Lazarus' illness will not end in his death. It is for the glory* of God. And so that people will know God's Son." So Jesus stayed where he was for two more days. Then Jesus and his disciples went to Bethany. Jesus said to his disciples, "Lazarus is asleep. I will go wake him up." The disciples did not understand that Lazarus had died.

Then Jesus arrived at Bethany. Lazarus had already died. He had been buried four days earlier. Martha went out to meet Jesus. She said, "Lord, if you had been here, my brother would not have died. But I know that God will do whatever you ask him." Jesus answered, "Your brother will live again. And I have the power to give people life. Anyone who believes in me will live for ever. Even if his body dies." Martha said, "I know this is true. I know you are God's Son, the Messiah*." Then Martha went home and told Mary.

Mary went out to meet Jesus. And the Jews* followed her. They were crying. When Jesus saw the Jews, he became very sad. Mary fell at Jesus' feet. She said, "Lord, if you had been here, my brother would not have died." Jesus asked, "Where have you put the body?" So they took Jesus to the cave where Lazarus' body was buried. And Jesus began to cry. He said, "Take the stone away." Then Jesus looked up towards the sky. He prayed, "Father, I thank you that you have listened to me. I want the people here to believe that you sent me." Then Jesus said in a loud voice, "Lazarus, come out!" Then Lazarus came out of the cave. And all of the people saw that Lazarus was alive. And many of them believed.

39

Ten Sick Men
Luke 17:11-19

Jesus and his disciples* began to walk to Jerusalem*. They walked on the road between Samaria* and Galilee*. On the road, they came to a village. They met 10 men there who had a bad illness of the skin. They had been sick for a long time. They saw Jesus and called out in a loud voice, "Master! Please be kind to us." Jesus knew they were sick. So Jesus said to them, "Go show yourselves to the priests*."

And all of the men obeyed Jesus. They began to walk to the Temple*. And while they were on the way, they were healed. Their sickness went away. One of the men was from Samaria. And he praised God in a loud voice. Immediately, he went to find Jesus. The man fell at Jesus' feet. He thanked him. Then Jesus asked, "Were not all 10 men made well? Did no one else come back to give praise to God except this Samaritan? Where are the other 9 men?"

Then Jesus said to the man, "Get up and go home. Your faith has made you well."

40

Two Men Pray

Luke 18:9–14

There were people in those days who thought they were very good. They thought that they were much better than other people. So Jesus told them a story. He said, "Two men went into the Temple* to pray. One man was a Pharisee*. And the other man gathered taxes from people. The Pharisee prayed, 'God, thank you that I am not like other men. They are bad people who do many bad things. And thank you, God, that I am not like that man. He takes taxes from people. But I give away one tenth of all that I have. And I do not eat for two days each week so that I can pray."

But the other man stood far away. He would not even look up to heaven*. He put his hands on his chest and cried. He prayed, 'God, please be kind to me. I know that I am a sinner*.'"

Then Jesus said, "Let me tell you about these men. When the man who took taxes left the Temple, he was now right with God. But when the Pharisee left the Temple, he was not right with God. People may think they are very important. But God will bring all of them down low. Other people know that they are humble. They know that they are not better than anyone else. And God will lift those people up to a good place."

41

Jesus and the Children
Matthew 19:13–15; Mark 10:13–16; Luke 18:15–17

During those days, crowds followed Jesus wherever he went. One day, people in the crowd began to bring little children to Jesus. They wanted Jesus to put his hands on their children and pray for them.

But Jesus' disciples* did not like this. They thought that Jesus had more important things to do than pray for little children. So the disciples told the people to stop. When Jesus heard this, he said to his disciples, "Let the little children come to me. Do not keep them away. God's kingdom* belongs to people like them."

Then Jesus took the children in his arms and blessed* them. And he said, "People must become like little children to come to me. If people do not become like little children, they cannot enter the kingdom of God."

42

Worker and Wages

Matthew 19:30–20:16

Everywhere Jesus went, he told stories. He used those stories to teach people things about this life and the life to come.

Just after Jesus blessed* a group of little children, Jesus said, "Many people who are first will be last. And many who are last will be first." But the people were not sure what he meant. So he told them another story.

Jesus said, "I will tell you what the kingdom* of heaven* is like. There was a man who owned a field where he grew grapes. Early one morning, he hired men to work in his field. He promised to give them one coin for a day's work. Then he sent them to work in the field.

"Later that same day, the man saw men in the market place. They had no work to do. So the man also brought them to his field to work. And he promised to pay them for their work. Then he sent them to work in the field. Two more times on that day, the man hired new workers. And he promised to pay them for their work. Then the day ended. And all of the workers went to be paid. The owner spoke to the worker in charge. 'First pay the men I hired last. Then pay the men I hired this morning.' So the man who owned the field paid every worker a full day's pay. But when the men who had worked all day saw this, they were very angry. They said, 'It is not fair. You paid them one coin too. We did more work than they did. We worked all day in the hot sun. But they only worked for a few hours.' But the man said, 'My friend, I am fair. I paid you what I promised. And now you have it. I chose to give the new men the same amount. It is my money. I do with it what I want. Why does that make you upset?'"

Then Jesus told the crowd what he meant. "Now you understand the saying. Those who are last will be first. And those who are first will be last."

43

Jesus and Bartimaeus*
Matthew 20:29-34; Mark 10:46-52; Luke 18:35-43

As Jesus traveled with his disciples*, he told them many things about himself. And the things that would happen to him. But the disciples did not understand what he was talking about.

Then one day, Jesus and his disciples were near Jericho*. A large crowd of people followed them. And they saw a blind man. He sat on the side of the road and begged for money and food. His name was Bartimaeus*.

The crowd told Bartimaeus, "Jesus of Nazareth* is about to walk by." So when Jesus walked by Bartimaeus, Bartimaeus shouted. "Jesus, Son of David*! Please be kind to me and help me!" Some people in the crowd told Bartimaeus to be quiet. But Bartimaeus shouted louder. "Master! Son of David! Please help me!" Then Jesus heard Bartimaeus. Jesus said to the crowd, "Bring that man to me." So some people from the crowd went to Bartimaeus. And they said, "Get up! Jesus wants you to come to him." So the blind man immediately went to Jesus.

Jesus asked, "What do you want me to do for you?" "Sir," Bartimaeus replied. "I want to see again." So Jesus said to Bartimaeus, "See again! You are healed because you believed." Immediately, Bartimaeus could see again. And he followed Jesus along the road. And Bartimaeus praised* God for what he had done. Many people in the crowd also saw what Jesus did. And they praised God too.

44

Zacchaeus*
Luke 19:1–10

Then Jesus and his disciples* went into Jericho*. They walked into the city. And there was a man named Zacchaeus* there. He was a leader of the men who collected taxes from the people. And he was very rich. Zacchaeus heard many amazing things about Jesus. And he wanted to see him. But Zacchaeus was a very short man. And he could not see Jesus because of the crowd. So Zacchaeus ran ahead of the crowd. Then he climbed up a tree.

When Jesus came by, he looked up and saw Zacchaeus. And Jesus said, "Zacchaeus, come down quickly. Today I will stay in your house." So Zacchaeus came down right away. He was happy to have Jesus come to his house.

But when the crowd of people heard this, they were not happy. They said, "Jesus has gone to the house of a man who has done many bad things." They did not understand why Jesus would do this. Then Zacchaeus stood up. He said, "Listen, Lord*! I will give half of my things to poor people. And I have taken too much money from some people. But I will give it back!"

So Jesus said, "Today God has saved* people in this house. I, the Son of Man*, came for people who are far away from God. I came to look for them and to save them."

Jesus Travels to Jerusalem*

The Triumphal Entry*
Matthew 21:1–11; Mark 11:1–10; Luke 19:29–44; John 12:12–19

As Jesus walked along the road with his disciples*, they came close to Jerusalem*. Many people were in Jerusalem for the Passover* feast.

Jesus and his disciples arrived on the hill called the Mount of Olives*. And Jesus sent out two of his disciples. He said to them, "Go to the village ahead. You will find a donkey's colt tied there. If anyone asks you, tell them that the Lord* needs it." Then the disciples did as Jesus told them. And they found the donkey's colt like Jesus had said.

They brought the donkey's colt back to Jesus. And the disciples placed their coats on its back. Jesus rode the donkey's colt into the city. A prophet* wrote about this long before: "Do not be afraid, people of Zion*. Look! Your King comes. He rides on a young donkey."

As people saw Jesus on the donkey's colt, they shouted. "We praise* you! Great is the king who comes with the name of the Lord God! God is good!" And the crowds of people laid their coats on the road before Jesus. And they carried palm branches as they shouted.

But some Pharisees* in the crowd said to Jesus, "Teacher, stop the crowds. These words are not right." But Jesus said to them, "If these people did not say them, the stones would shout them."

Then Jesus was near the city. He looked at the city, and he cried. He knew that the people did not really understand who he was.

When he came into the city, many people did not know what was happening. So they asked, "Who is this man?" And the crowd answered, "This is the prophet, Jesus. He is from Nazareth* of Galilee*."

But when the Pharisees saw this, it troubled them. "Look," they said. "The people are leaving us to follow him."

46

Jesus Cleanses the Temple*
Matthew 21:12-17; Mark 11:15-18; Luke 19:45-46

The next day, after he had come to Jerusalem*, Jesus went to the Temple*. When he looked around, he saw people who were buying and selling things. They sold many kinds of animals. There were other people who sat at tables to change coins for people. Jesus became very angry when he saw this. He made a whip out of rope. And he made all the people and their animals leave. Then Jesus pushed over the tables. And he said to the people who sold birds: "Take them out of here! Do not make my Father's house into a market! The Lord* said in the Scriptures*, 'My house will be called a house where people from all nations can pray. But you have made it a place for robbers!'"

After this, blind people and people who could not walk came to the Temple to see Jesus. He healed many people there. When he did, people began to shout praise* to him. Children sang, "Praise to the son of David*!" When the leaders in the Temple saw this, they became angry. "Do you hear what these children are saying?," they asked.

"Yes," Jesus said. "Have you never read what the Scriptures* say? 'You, Lord, have called the children, even the little children, to offer praise.'"

The Widow's Small Coin

Mark 12:38-44; Luke 21:1-4

Soon after he made the sellers leave the Temple*, Jesus came back to Jerusalem*. For many days, he went to the Temple to teach. Jesus took his disciples* with him. He wanted them to see what he did and hear what he would say.

As he watched crowds of people go in and out of the Temple, Jesus said, "Be careful. And watch the teachers of the law*. They wear long robes. They love when people see the things that they do. They think they are the most important people in all of the Temple. They do this so that others will think they are important. But God will punish these men."

While Jesus spoke to the crowds, he was standing in the Temple. And he saw there was a box for money there. People put money there to make gifts for the Temple. Many rich people put money into the box. They were very proud. They wanted other people to see them put money into the box. Then Jesus saw a woman come to the box. She was alone. Jesus knew her husband had died. And she was very poor. Then she put two small coins in the money box.

Then Jesus said, "Listen to this. This poor woman put a greater gift into that money box than the rich people. The rich people have plenty of money. But they only gave a small amount of what they have. But this poor woman has almost no money. She gave everything she had. It was all she had to live on."

48

The Women and the Lamps
Matthew 25:1-13

Jesus told the crowds many stories, during his time in Jerusalem*. On this day, he would tell them another one.

Jesus said, "I will tell you what the kingdom* of God is like. There were ten young women who were going to a marriage party. So they took their lamps with them. The women were going to meet a man who was to be married to a wife. Five young women were very clever. But the other five women were silly.

Ten women waited for the man. The silly women waited with their lamps. But they did not have any extra oil. The clever women also waited with their lamps. But they did bring extra oil with them. And the man did not come for a long time. The ten women became very tired. And they fell asleep.

At midnight, someone cried out, "Here is the man who is to be married. Come out to meet him!" So the women woke up and began to get their lamps ready. But the silly women did not have enough oil to keep their lamps burning. So they said to the clever women, 'Give us some of your oil. Our lamps are going out.' But the clever women said, 'No. Then we will not have enough oil. You must go get your own.' So the silly women went to find more oil. While they were away, the man who was to be married came. The clever women were ready and went with him into the house. And the servants shut the door.

When the silly women arrived, they came to the house. But the doors were closed. So they shouted, 'Sir, please let us in!' But the man said, 'Go away. I do not know you.'"

Then Jesus said, "So you must watch carefully. Because you do not know the day or the hour when the Son of Man* will return."

49

Three Servants
Matthew 25:14-30; Luke 19:12-27

Jesus came back to Jerusalem* day after day. Crowds came to listen to him. So did many of the leaders of the Jews*. During those days, Jesus answered many questions. And he told them many new stories.

"I will tell you what the kingdom* of heaven* is like. A master went on a journey. But before the master left, he told his servants to come to him. The master said, 'Take care of what I have while I am away. Put my money to work.' So the master gave the first servant five bags of money. To the second, he gave two bags. To the last servant, he gave one bag. Then the master left.

After a long time away, the master came home. He asked his servants what they had done with his money. The first servant said, "Master, you gave me five bags. I used them to earn five more." The master said to that servant, "You have done well. I will now put you in charge of many things." The second servant said, "Master, you gave me two bags of money. With it, I have earned two more." The master said to that servant, "You did well. Now I will let you care for even more."

Then the last servant said, 'Master, I know what you are like. I know that you have a lot of power. I was afraid. And I buried your money in the ground. Look! I have all of your money. I have not lost any of it.'

But the master was very angry with this servant. He said to him, 'You are bad and lazy. If you really knew me, you should have put my money in the bank. Then you would at least be able to give me my money plus some extra money.' Then the master took the bag of money from that servant. And he gave it to the servant who had ten bags. Then the master said, 'People who use what they have, will be given more. But those who do not use what they have, even what they have will be taken from them.'"

50

Jesus Washes the Disciple*s' Feet
Matthew 26:17-19; Mark 14:12-16; Luke 22: 7-16; John 13:1-17

Now it was the day when the Jewish* people sacrificed* a lamb for the Passover*. Jesus' disciples* went to him. "Lord*," they said. "Where do you want us to prepare for you to eat the special Passover meal?" Jesus said, "Go into the city. You will meet a certain man. Tell him, 'The Teacher says, 'My time is near. I want to have the special Passover meal at your house with my disciples.'" So the disciples obeyed Jesus. And they found the man like Jesus said. They prepared the special Passover meal.

Then it was time to eat the meal. Jesus said, "I am very happy to eat this special meal with you." Then Jesus stood up. He took off his coat. And he tied a piece of cloth around himself. Then he poured water into a bowl and began to wash his disciples' feet. Jesus dried their feet with the cloth that was around him. When Jesus did this, it surprised his disciples.

Then Jesus came to Simon Peter* to wash his feet. But Simon Peter said, "Lord, will you really wash my feet?" Jesus said, "You do not understand what I am doing. But you will soon understand." Simon Peter answered, "Then, Lord, wash my hands and head too!" Then Jesus said, "I need only to wash your feet. All of you are clean, except one of you." Jesus said this because he already knew that Judas* would give him to his enemies.

When Jesus had washed all the disciples' feet, he returned to the table. Jesus said, "I have given you an example. You should do for others what I have just done for you. No servant is more important than his master. Now go and serve others."

51

The Last Supper

Matthew 26:20-29; Mark 14:17-26; Luke 22:17-20

As they ate together, Jesus said, "One of you will betray me to my enemies." This made the disciples* very sad. They did not understand. They asked Jesus, "Lord*, I will not betray you. Will I?" But Jesus said, "The one who dips into the bowl with me will betray me. And it will all happen just like it is written in the Scriptures*. But it will be very bad for that man. He will wish he was never born."

Then Jesus took bread. He gave thanks to God. And he broke the bread. Jesus said, "Take this and eat it. This is my body." Then Jesus took a cup. He gave thanks to God. And he handed the cup to his disciples. Jesus said, "All of you drink. This is the blood of my special promise. My blood is to forgive* the wrong things of many people. Listen. I will not eat this meal with you again until we are all in my Father's kingdom*." And after they finished the Passover meal, Jesus sang a special song with his disciples. Then they all went to the Mount of Olives*.

52

Judas* Betrays Jesus

Matthew 26:14–16, 23–25, 36–50; 27:3-10; Mark 14:10-11; 32-45;
Luke 22:1-6: 47-53; John 13:26-30; 18:1-5; Acts 1:18-19

Days before the Passover*, Judas* went before the priests*. He asked, "What will you give me if I betray Jesus?" They agreed to give him 30 coins.

Days later, as they ate the Passover meal together, Jesus told his disciples* that one of them would betray him. This troubled them. They did not know who Jesus was talking about. So Jesus said, "The man who dips into the bowl with me will betray me." As they ate, Jesus dipped a piece of bread into a bowl. Then he gave it to Judas. As soon as Judas took the bread, Satan* went into him. Then Jesus said, "What you are about to do, do quickly." And Judas went out of the room. But the other disciples did not know what Judas was doing.

After they ate together, Jesus took his disciples to the Mount of Olives*. The Mount of Olives was just outside of Jerusalem*. They came to a garden there. Jesus said to them, "Sit here while I go pray." Jesus took Peter*, James*, and John* with him. Then Jesus became very sad. He said, "I feel as if I could die because I am so sad. Wait here and stay awake." Then Jesus walked further.

When Jesus was alone, he fell on the ground. He prayed, "My Father, you can do all things. Please take away what is before me. But do not do what I want. Do what you want." Then Jesus went back to Peter, James, and John. But they were asleep. Jesus said to them, "Why do you sleep? Could you not even stay awake for one hour?" Then Jesus went to pray again. When he returned for the third time, Jesus said, "Do not sleep now! Look! It is time. The Son of Man* will be given to sinners*. Get up! They are very close."

When he said this, Judas came. A large crowd was with him. The chief priest had sent them. Judas had told the crowd, "Arrest the man that I kiss." So, Judas went to Jesus and kissed him. Then Jesus said to Judas, "Do you betray the Son of Man with a kiss?" And the crowd arrested Jesus.

Peter* Denies Jesus

Matthew 26:31-35, 69-75; Mark 14:66-72; Luke 22:54-62;
John 18:15-18, 25-27; 21:15-25

Now before the men took Jesus away, he was still in the garden with his disciples*. Jesus looked at his disciples and said, "Tonight you will all leave because of me. It is written in the Scriptures*: 'I will strike down the shepherd*. And the sheep will leave.' But do not be afraid. I will be alive again." Then Peter* said, "Lord*. The others may leave you. But I never will." Jesus said, "Peter, it will happen tonight. Before a rooster crows, three times you will tell people that you do not know me." This made Peter very sad. So he said, "I would die with you, Lord. I would never say I do not know you." And the other disciples agreed with Peter.

Then the crowd came to arrest Jesus. And they took him away. And everything that Jesus said happened. Peter followed the crowd. But he did not go too close.

Peter sat outside of the chief priest's* house. A woman came to Peter. She said, "You were with Jesus!" But Peter said, "No I was not." Then Peter left the yard. He went to the gate. Another woman saw Peter. She said, "This man was with Jesus!" But Peter spoke very strongly. And he said, "I do not know him!" Later, some people went to Peter. They said, "You must have been with Jesus. You talk like he did." This made Peter very angry. He spoke very strongly again. Peter said, "I told you! I do not know Jesus!" Immediately, a rooster crowed. Then Peter remembered Jesus' words. And he went outside and cried and cried.

54

The Trial before the Sanhedrin*
Matthew 26:36-68; Mark 14:32-65; Luke 22:39-53; John 18:1-14, 19-24

After the men arrested Jesus, the men took him to Caiaphas*, the chief priest*. They wanted to show that Jesus had done something wrong. But they knew Jesus had done nothing wrong. They wanted someone to say bad things about Jesus, even if they had to lie. They wanted to find a reason to put Jesus to death.

While he stood there, they asked Jesus many questions. They asked about Jesus' disciples*. And they asked about the things Jesus had taught. But Jesus did not speak. This made them very angry. Then Jesus said, "You know what I have done. You know that I have done no wrong thing."

Then the chief priest said, "All right, tell us this. Are you the Messiah*? Are you the Son of God*?" And Jesus answered, "It is as you have said. Now listen. You will see the Son of Man* sitting at God's right hand. And you will see him, the Son of Man, come on the clouds of heaven*." Then Caiaphas tore his clothes in anger. He said, "This man has spoken an evil thing against God! " And he turned to the others and asked, "What is your judgment? What do you say?" And they all answered, "He deserves to die!" And they spit on him and hit him and slapped his face.

55

The Trial before Pilate*

Matthew 27:11-26; Mark 15:1-15; Luke 23:1-25; John 18:28-19:15

The chief priests* and the men who worked for them hated Jesus. They wanted to kill him. So they tied Jesus with ropes. And they took Jesus to Pilate*. The Jewish* leaders told Pilate that Jesus had done many wrong things. So Pilate asked Jesus, "Are you the king of the Jews*?" Jesus answered, "You have said it." Pilate said, "Have you heard the many bad things the Jews said you have done?" But Jesus did not answer Pilate. And this surprised him.

Each year during the Passover* festival, Pilate let one prisoner go free. And Pilate let a crowd of people choose who would go free. There was a prisoner named Barabbas*. He was a very bad man. So Pilate asked the people, "Do you want me to let the king of the Jews go free?" Pilate knew the Jewish* leaders were jealous of Jesus. And the Jewish leaders told the crowd, "Ask Pilate to let Barabbas go free." So they did. Then Pilate asked the people again, "What should I do to Jesus? This man who is the king of the Jews." The people shouted at Pilate: "Kill him on a cross*!"

But Pilate's wife sent a message to him. She said, "You should let Jesus go. He has done nothing wrong. I had a dream* about this." So Pilate said to the people, "Why do you want Jesus to die? What has he done wrong?" But the people shouted even louder. "Kill him on a cross!" So Pilate washed his hands in front of the people. And he said, "You are Jesus' killers. Not me." But the people shouted at Pilate, "We do not care! We will take the blame." So Pilate let Barabbas go. Pilate had Jesus whipped. Then Pilate sent Jesus to be nailed to a cross. Soldiers put a king's robe on Jesus. And they took some very sharp branches and made a crown for him. They put the crown on Jesus' head. And they laughed at Jesus and hit him.

The Crucifixion* and Burial
Matthew 27:27-66; Mark 15:16-47; Luke 23:26-56; John 19:16-42

After Pilate* decided to have Jesus nailed to a cross*, he called soldiers to take Jesus away. The soldiers spit on Jesus and hit him many times. They took the robe off Jesus. They put Jesus' own clothes on him. Then they made Jesus carry a large cross* made of wood.

As they walked, the soldiers saw a man near the road. His name was Simon*. The soldiers made Simon help Jesus carry the cross. They went to a place called Golgotha*. This word means "Place of the Skull" in the Jewish language. There was a large crowd of people who followed them there. Some of the women began to cry. But Jesus said to them, "Do not cry because of me. Cry for yourselves and for your children because of this."

Then the soldiers made a strong drink. And they tried to force Jesus to drink it. But he would not drink it. Then the soldiers nailed Jesus to the cross. They took his clothes and played games to decide who would take them. Then they made a sign that said "This is Jesus, the king of the Jews*." They placed the sign at the top of the cross. And the Jewish* leaders laughed at Jesus. There were two men on crosses beside Jesus. They were robbers.

It was midday. But the sky became dark for three hours. The sun was dark. Then Jesus asked for a drink. Then Jesus said in a loud voice, "It is finished." And after he said this, Jesus died. And the curtain in the Temple* tore in half.

The next day was an important day in the Passover* week. So the Jews asked Pilate to take the men down from the crosses. The soldiers put a spear in Jesus' side to make sure that he was dead. And blood and water came out of Jesus' side. Then a rich man came from the town of Arimathea*. His name was Joseph*. He was a follower* of Jesus. Joseph went to Pilate and asked for Jesus' body. Then Joseph wrapped Jesus' body in a cloth. Joseph put Jesus' body in a special cave cut in a rock. And they rolled a large stone in front of the cave to close it.

Jesus is Raised
and Ascends

57

The Resurrection*

Matthew 28:1-10; Mark 16:1-11; Luke 24:1-12; John 20:1-18

Now when the Sabbath* was over, Mary Magdalene* and the other Mary* went to the cave where Jesus was buried. It was very early on the first day of the week. But they saw that the large stone was not in front of the cave. Then an angel* from the Lord* appeared to them. The angel said, "Don't be afraid. I know you are looking for Jesus. But Jesus is not here. He is alive again. Come and see! This cave is empty. Now go tell Jesus' disciples*!"

The women were afraid, and they were very happy too. So they ran to tell the disciples.

When the women found the disciples, they told them what they had seen. The cave was empty, and Jesus was alive again. But the disciples did not believe the women. They thought the women were telling them a silly story. But Peter* and John* got up and went to the cave. John bent down and looked inside. He saw that it was empty. Jesus' body was not there. Peter saw this too. But they did not yet understand what had happened. So they returned to the place where they were staying.

But Mary Magdalene stood outside the tomb. She was crying. When she looked into the cave, she saw two angels. They asked, "Why are you crying?" She answered, "They have taken my Lord away, and I don't know where they have put him." Then she turned around and there, in front of her, was Jesus. But she thought he was the man who took care of the garden. Jesus said, "Why are you crying? Who are you looking for?" "Sir," she said. "If you have taken Jesus from here, tell me where you have put him."

Then Jesus said to her, "Mary." She turned to him and said, "Teacher!" And Jesus said, "Go to my brothers. Tell them I will go up to my Father and your Father; my God and Your God."

So Mary ran and told the disciples, "I have seen the Lord!"

The Road to Emmaus*

Luke 24:13-35

It was the first day of the week. Some women had told the disciples* that they had seen Jesus. Peter and John* had gone to the cave where Jesus was buried. And his body was not there, just as the women had said.

Later that day, two of his disciples went to the village, Emmaus*. They were walking. And they were very sad. They talked about Jesus as they walked. But then Jesus himself came to them. And he walked along with them. The men saw Jesus. But they did not know who he was. God kept this from them. So Jesus asked them, "What are you talking about?"

They stood still. One of them was named Cleopas*. And Cleopas answered, "Many things happened in Jerusalem* in the last few days. How is it that you have not heard about these things?" Then Jesus asked, "What things have happened?"

They said, "We are talking about Jesus who was from Nazareth*. He was a prophet* from God. He did many good things. And he spoke God's words with great power. But he was killed on a cross*. Before, we hoped that he would save* Israel*. We hoped that he would make us free again. Today is the third day since he died. Early this morning, some women said that he is not dead. But no one has seen Jesus."

Then Jesus said, "Why are you so slow to believe? Do you not remember what the prophets said? The Messiah* would have to die? Only then could he show his glory.*" Then Jesus explained the Scriptures* to them. He told them how the Scriptures spoke about him. When they came to the village, it was almost dark. So they asked Jesus to stay the night. Jesus went with them and ate with them. And as Jesus ate, the disciples' eyes became clear. They understood that the one they had walked with was Jesus. And as soon as they understood this, they could not see him anymore. He was gone.

So they hurried back to Jerusalem to find the disciples. They were all very happy when they heard the news.

59

Thomas* Doubts

Luke 24:36-49; John 20:19-29

When the men came back from Emmaus*, Jesus' disciples* were in a house together. They talked about the things that happened before Jesus was killed. But they locked the door because they were afraid of the Jewish* leaders. As they talked, Jesus came to them. And he stood with them. Jesus' disciples were surprised and very afraid. But Jesus said, "Peace*. Do not be afraid." He showed them his hands and his side. This amazed* the disciples and filled them with joy. Then Jesus asked for something to eat. After he ate with them, Jesus said, "I told you about all the things that would happen to me. Everything that Moses* and the prophets* wrote about me has happened. They wrote that the Messiah* would suffer. And that he would rise from the dead. Those who follow him will preach* in his name. They will call people to turn from their sins*. They will begin in Jerusalem*. Then people from every nation will hear the message. Now, as my Father sent me, so I send you." After he had said these things, Jesus left them.

Now one of the disciples was not with them when Jesus came into the house. His name was Thomas*. Because he had not seen Jesus, he did not believe the other disciples. Eight days later, the disciples were all together again. This time, Thomas was there too. And just as he had before, Jesus came into the room. "Peace be with you," Jesus said. And then he looked at Thomas and said, "Do not be afraid. It is really me. See. Look at my hands and my feet. Touch me! Then you will know and be sure and believe." And Thomas looked at Jesus and answered, "My Lord* and my God." Then Jesus said, "You believe because you have seen me. But many people will believe in me even though they have not seen me."

60

The Ascension*

Matthew 28:16-20; Luke 24:50-53; Acts 1:1-11

Jesus was alive. He showed himself to his disciples* and taught them for 40 days. During those days, five hundred people saw him. While he was with them, he told them not to leave Jerusalem*. They were to wait there for the Father's promise - the Holy Spirit*. Then he gathered them together at the place where they had agreed to meet.

Then Jesus held up his hands and prayed for the disciples. Jesus said to them, "God has given me all of the power in heaven* and on earth. So you must go into the whole world. Teach everyone to follow me. Baptize* the people who believe, in the name of the Father, the Son, and the Holy Spirit. Teach them to obey what I have taught you. And remember this. I will always be with you, until the very end."

Then Jesus told the disciples that God would send them a helper, the Holy Spirit. He would help them to obey Jesus' last words. After Jesus spoke to them, God took him up to heaven. The disciples saw this happen. And they were so amazed*. They praised God for this. Then the disciples went back to Jerusalem. They went to the Temple* there and praised* God for all that he had done. And they did what Jesus told them to do.

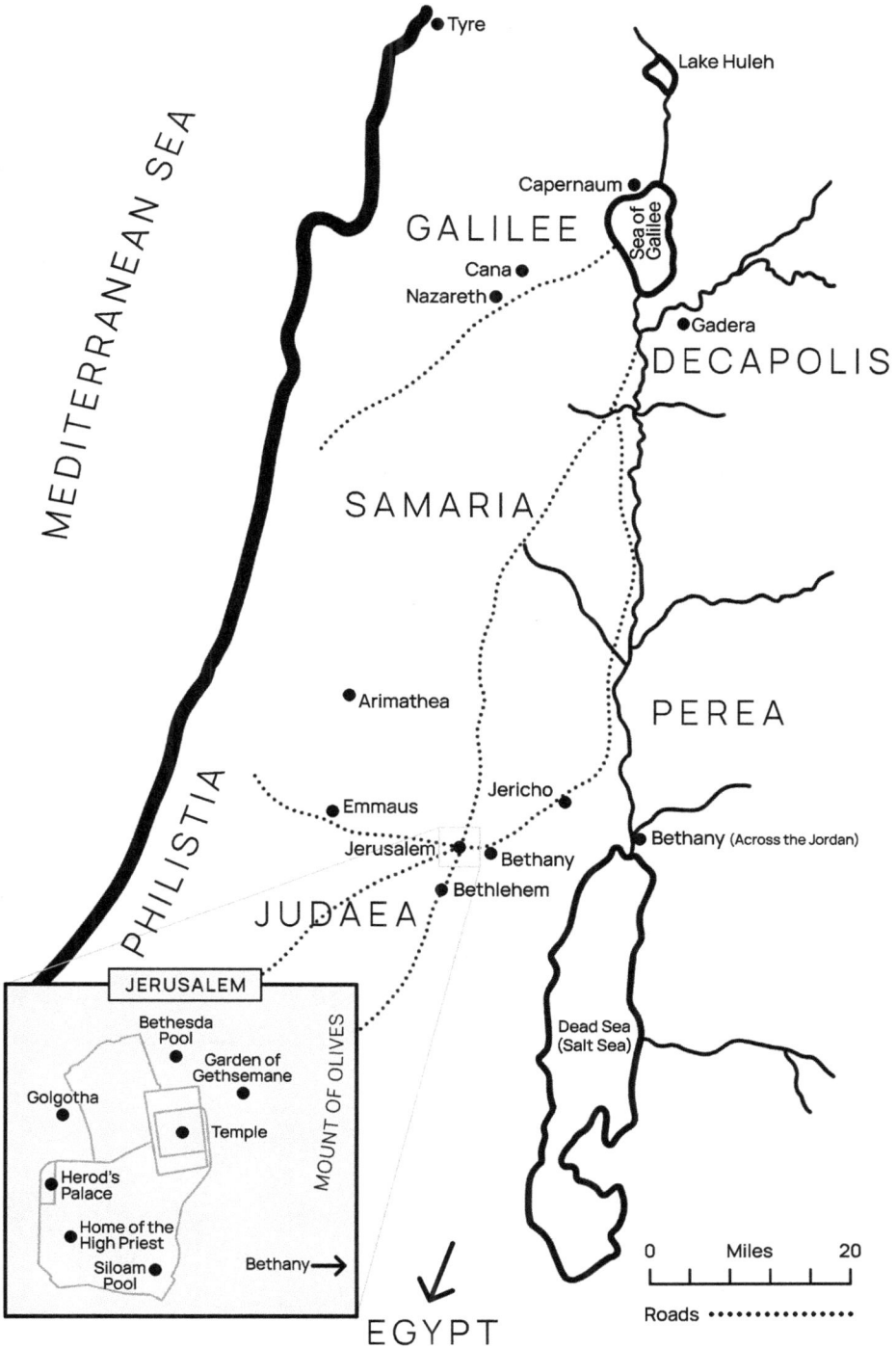

Simple Stories from the Life of Jesus
(A Leader's Guide)

HOW TO USE THESE STORIES

Since we first wrote these stories, we have found that people use them in many different ways. Some read the stories to learn more about Jesus. Some learn and share the stories with people who do not know the story of Jesus' life. Some people meet in groups to learn the stories and talk about them together. Some use the stories to help people learn English. Sometimes they meet with just one person. Sometimes they meet in small groups. Here are a few ideas that may help you as you read the stories.

A Leader's Guide

How to Use the Stories with One Person

APPENDIX ONE

Pray.

Ask God to help you understand the story.

Read the story out loud.

Or, the leader can learn the story well enough to tell the story.

First, ask questions that can help you **REMEMBER** the story:

    a. Who are the people in the story?

    b. Does anyone speak in the story? What do the characters say?

    c. What happens in the story?

    d. In what order do things happen? (What happens first? Second? Next?)

Now, ask the other person to retell the story, if possible. The leader can help fill in what is missing..

Next, ask questions that can help you **UNDERSTAND** the story:

    a. What did you like about the story? What was your favorite part of the story?

    b. What part of the story was hard to understand?

    c. Was there anything that made you feel uncomfortable?

    d. What does the story tell you about God or Jesus?

    e. What does the story tell you about people?

    f. What questions do you still have?

Read the story again.

Now, ask questions that can help you **BENEFIT** from the story:

   a. How does the story apply to you? What can you learn from the story?

   b. What does this story encourage you to think about in a new way?

   c. Will you make any changes in your life after reading this story? What are they?

Last, ask questions that will help you **SHARE** this story with others:

   a. Do you know anyone who might need to hear this story?

   b. How could you tell them about it?

   c. How can you pray for them?

How to Use the Stories with a Story Group
APPENDIX TWO

Pray.

Ask God to help you understand the story.

Listen to the story.

Or, the leader can learn the story well enough to tell the story.

First, ask questions that can help you **REMEMBER** the story:

    a. Who are the people in the story?

    b. Does anyone speak in the story? What do the characters say?

    c. What happens in the story?

    d. In what order do things happen? (What happens first? Second? Next?)

Read or tell the story again.

Next, ask questions that can help you **UNDERSTAND** the story:

    a. What did you like about the story? What was your favorite part of the story?

    b. What part of the story was hard to understand?

    c. Was there anything that made you feel uncomfortable?

    d. What does the story tell you about God or Jesus?

    e. What does the story tell you about people?

    f. What questions do you still have?

Tell the story again.

This time, ask one of the students to try to tell the story. The teacher and members of the class can help them as they try to tell the story if they need help.

Now, ask questions that can help you **BENEFIT** from the story:

a. How does the story apply to you? What can you learn from the story?

b. What does this story encourage you to think about in a new way?

c. Will you make any changes in your life after reading this story? What are they?

Last, ask questions that will help you **SHARE** this story with others:

a. Do you know anyone who might need to hear this story?

b. How could you tell them about it?

c. How can you pray for them?

After working through the story three times and answering the questions, give each member of the group a written copy of the story. They can take the story with them and learn it. At the next group meeting, each person can take a turn telling the story.

How to Use the Stories to Teach English

APPENDIX THREE

The teacher welcomes and greets the students.

The students are asked to introduce themselves.

Then they are asked to tell about something that happened during their week. (What was the most interesting thing that happened? Or what was the most confusing thing that happened? Or what happened that made them the happiest?)

The teacher may want to review some vocabulary words from a previous week.

The teacher will then introduce the new story.

Pray.

Ask God to help you understand the story.

Read the story out loud.

Or, the teacher can learn the story well enough to tell the story.

First, ask questions that can help you **REMEMBER** the story:

  a. Who are the people in the story?
  b. Does anyone speak in the story? What do the characters say?
  c. What happens in the story?
  d. In what order do things happen? (What happens first? Second? Next?)

Read or tell the story again.

Next, ask questions that can help you **UNDERSTAND** the story:

  a. What did you like about the story? What was your favorite part of the story?

  b. What part of the story was hard to understand?

  c. Was there anything that made you feel uncomfortable?

  d. What does the story tell you about God or Jesus?

  e. What does the story tell you about people?

  f. What questions do you still have?

Read or tell the story again.

This time, ask one of the students to try to tell the story. The teacher and members of the class can help them as they try to tell the story if they need help.

Now, ask questions that can help you **BENEFIT** from the story:

  a. How does the story apply to you? What can you learn from the story?

  b. What does this story encourage you to think about in a new way?

Last, ask questions that will help you **SHARE** this story with others:

  a. Do you know anyone who might need to hear this story?

  b. How could you tell them about it?

After working through the story three times and answering the questions, give each member of the group a written copy of the story. They can take the story with them and learn it. At the next group meeting, each person can take a turn telling the story. This will help the student practice speaking in a group. This can also be used as a pronunciation exercise.

WORD LIST

This Word List will help you better understand these stories. Any word in the book with a * beside it is defined in this list. Sometimes, a word can have more than one meaning. This list will include the meanings that help you understand what you read.

Abraham Abraham is the father of all of the Jews. His name was Abram. Then, God changed Abram's name to Abraham. God made a promise to him. He said that Abraham's family would become a great nation. God would bless* all of the other nations through one of his children.

Altar A special table for people to burn animals or other gifts which they offer to God.

Amazed When a person is surprised or confused when they see something or hear something that they did not expect.

Andrew One of Jesus' disciples. He was the brother of the disciple Simon Peter.

Anoint To mark a person with oil to show that God has chosen them; someone that the Holy Spirit* has chosen.

Anna Anna was an elderly widow in Jerusalem. She worshiped God with regular fasting and praying. She was also one of the first people to understand that the baby Jesus was God's promised Messiah. Anna was also one of the few women in the Bible to be called a prophetess.

Angel An angel is a spirit* being. God created* them to serve him. Sometimes, he used the angels to carry a message for him. God made so many angels that we can not count them. But not all of the angels followed God. Some of them turned away from him. They became the enemies of God. They became known as evil* spirits*. Satan* is their leader. Some day, God will throw Satan* and his angels into a fire that never goes out.

Apostle An Apostle was a man sent to speak for Jesus. Jesus chose these men. Each of them spent time with Jesus. Each of them saw Jesus after he came back from death. God used them to start his church*and give us the New Testament*. A person sent to bring a message.

Arimathea The town where Joseph, a follower of Jesus, lived. Joseph cared for Jesus' body after his death.

Ascension When Christ's body passed from earth to heaven.*

Baptize/Baptism A teacher or leader puts someone under the water for a moment. Then the person is brought up from the water. In this way we show that we believe the message. We have turned from our sin*. God has made us clean. After Jesus rose from the grave, this was the way to show that we belong to Christ and his church*.

Barabbas Barabbas was a prisoner in Jerusalem when Jesus came to the city for the last time. He was supposed to die because of what he had done. Pilate offered to let Jesus go free, but the crowd asked that Barabbus be set free instead. The crowd called for Jesus to go to die on a cross.

Bartholomew One of Jesus' disciples.

Bartimeaus Bartimeaus was a blind man who lived near the town of Jericho. He was a beggar. When he heard that Jesus was passing by where he was, he called out to him. Jesus healed his eyes so that he could see again.

Believe To follow something that you are sure is true; to trust someone; to have confidence in someone. I trust someone when I depend on what they say to be true.

Believer A believer is a person who knows and trusts Christ.

Bethany A town in Judea near Jerusalem. Bethany was the home of Jesus' friends Mary, Martha, and Lazarus.

Bethesda A pool of water in Jerusalem. Many sick people lay around the pool. They waited for the water in the pool to move. They all believed that an angel* would come down to the pool and move the water. The first person to go into the pool would be made well.

Bethlehem Bethlehem was the village south of Jerusalem. David was born there. Jesus was born there as well.

Bless/Bless/Blessing - to say or do something good for someone; to speak well of someone; to give things to someone to honor them; to ask God to do good to someone; to call for good things to happen to someone; to set someone apart for special benefit; the good things God does for us. When we ask God to help us receive good things, we are asking for blessings.

Caiaphas Caiaphus was the Jewish high priest during the years of Jesus' ministry. He was the one who organized the plot to kill Jesus. He was the one who led the trial of Jesus before the Jewish counsel.

Cana A town in Galilee.

Capernaum Capernaum was a city on the northwest shore of the Sea of Galilee. Capernaum was the chosen home city of Jesus after he was driven from Nazareth by the Jewish leaders. Capernaum was also the home of Peter and Andrew and where Jesus called them to follow him. Jesus also found Matthew, a tax collector in Capernaum.

Cesar Augustus Caesar was the title for the king of the Romans. The Bible mentions many of these men. Caesar Augustus was the king who was in control when Jesus was born.

Christ Christ is a title that is used to name Jesus. It means 'the chosen one'. It is a way that the early Christians said that Jesus was the Messiah,* the One God had chosen.

Church The church is a group of people that follow and believe all about Jesus Christ. They meet together. They baptize* believers.* They eat the Lord's Supper. They obey the teachings of Christ

Circumcise/Circumcision To cut off the skin that covers the end of the sex part of a boy or a man; a mark for Israelites* to show that a man agreed to obey God's rules; a mark of a good and clean spirit.*

Cleopas Cleopas was a follower of Jesus during his ministry. He was among the few who saw the Lord on the day of his resurrection. He was one of the two men who saw the risen Lord on the road to Emmaus.

Creation/Created When God made the world and everything there is; everything that God has made; what God did when he made everything from nothing.

Cross Two pieces of wood fixed together. The Romans punished people by fixing them to a cross to die. Jesus died this way; to carry your cross means not to put yourself first but to put Jesus and other people first in your life.

Crucifixion When they killed someone by nailing the body to a cross*; the death of Jesus when they nailed him to the cross.*

David David was the king of all of Israel*. God made a promise to David. He told David that one of his son's would be king for ever. Jesus was sometimes called the son of David because he was from David's family line.

Devil Another name for Satan*. Satan is the worst of the evil* spirits. The Devil is the enemy of God and his people.

Disciple A person who wants to do the same things as another person and learn from them; one who follows another and learns from him; a person who believes in Jesus and follows the things he teaches.

Disobey To not obey; to not do what God tells you.

Dream A vision that someone can have while they are awake or alseep. In the Bible, God uses visions and dreams to speak to his people. God gave the prophets* visions to show what he wanted them to say to the people. Not all dreams or visions come from God.

Egypt Egypt was a land to the south of Israel. The sons of Jacob lived in Egypt for many years until Moses came to lead them out. When Jesus was a small boy, his family went there for a while.

Elijah Elijah was a prophet*. He spoke for God to the people of Israel*. The king did not like Elijah. The queen did not like him either. But God watched over him. He did many wonders in Israel*. He overcame many of the prophets*of the false god Baal.

Elisha Elisha was a prophet*. For many years, he helped Elijah. When Elijah went to be with God, Elisha took his place. He did many wonders in the land. God gave him great power.

Elizabeth Elizabeth had a son in her old age. She named him John. He became a prophet*. One day, he baptized* Jesus. She was related to Mary, the mother of Jesus. Mary went to visit her before she gave birth to Jesus.

Emmaus Emmaus was a town where Jesus appeared to two men after he rose from the dead. The men were on their way to Emmaus when Jesus joined them on the road. This road connected Emmaus to Jerusalem.

Eternal things that have always been and will always continue to be; a thing that has no beginning or ending; a thing that never changes; things that continue for ever.

Evil Bad; the opposite of good; wicked; doing bad; things that hurt someone.

Evil One Another name for Satan.* He is the one who works against God and God's people. The Evil One is sometimes called the Devil.

Evil spirit A bad spirit* who works for Satan* and does bad things; a spirit that works against God and his people.

Faith Faith means to believe in someone or something. To trust* and believe in God. To know that God is real, even when we cannot see him.

Fast/Fasting When people choose not to eat any food for a time. They might fast to help them to think about God or to help them to pray.

Follower to go after someone who leads; the men and women who believe in Jesus and do what he says.

Forgive/forgiven/forgiveness - to show mercy* and not to remember bad things against someone; to set someone free from wrong things that they do; to let someone go free from punishment. When God forgives us, he does not hold the wrong things we do against us.

Frankincense A precious oil; the wise men gave frankincense to the baby Jesus as a gift.

Gabriel Gabriel was an angel who spoke for God many times in the scriptures. He spoke to the prophet* Daniel in the Old Testament. And he spoke to both Mary and Joseph, sent by God to announce the birth of Jesus.

Gadara/Gadarene Gadara was a city near the shore of the Sea of Galilee. The people who lived there were called the Gadarene people.

Galilee Galilee was located in the northern part of Israel. In Jesus' day Galilee was part of the Roman Empire. One of the three provinces of Israel, it included the whole northern section of the country. The Jordan River and Sea of Galilee formed the Eastern border of Galilee. Jesus grew up in Nazareth, one of the cities in Galilee. Jesus did most of his ministry in the towns and villages in Galilee.

Gentiles Gentile was the name given to any people that were not Jews. No matter what nation the people came from, if they were not Jews, they were called Gentiles. People who did not know the God of the Jews.

Gethsemane A garden outside Jerusalem* where Jesus prayed before his death; where Judas* betrayed Jesus.

Glory Everything that makes God beautiful and great; like a great king; a bright light from God or Jesus.

Golgotha The place where Jesus was killed on a cross. "Golgotha" means "Place of the Skull" in the Jewish* language.

Gospel The good news for everybody that God saves people from sin* through Jesus Christ; the good news of the things Jesus has done for us by his life, death and rising from the dead; the message from God to us; the four books at the beginning of the New Testament.

Grace Grace is a gift of God that we do not deserve because of the bad things that we have done. Grace is what God gives because he is so kind to us. The forgiveness* and help that comes from God.

Heaven The place where God and Christ are; the future home of the people who know God; the place of happiness and peace* where God lives and rules; the place where people who know God and Jesus will go after they die; the sky God made.

Herod Herod was the ruler of Israel at the time of Jesus' birth. He ruled under the authority given to him by Rome. He was a great builder, who rebuilt the Temple in Jerusalem. He was also the one who ordered that all of the male children in Bethlehem be killed. Joseph and Mary fled to Egypt to escape the anger of Herod.

Herodias Herodias was the wife of Herod Antipas and had been the wife of Herod's brother, Philip. John the Baptist spoke against this marriage. Herodias was the woman who caused the death of John the Baptist.

Holy, holiness What God is like; different and better than all other things; all good with no bad in it; a thing that God has; separate from sin*; clean.

Holy Spirit The Holy Spirit is God, as is God the Father and God the Son. Jesus promised to send the Holy Spirit to all that know him as the Son of God. Nobody sees the Holy Spirit, but he joins with the spirit of those that know Jesus. The Holy Spirit helps a person to follow Jesus and to do good things.

Hope To look for a future thing that God had promised.

Immanuel A name for Jesus meaning 'God with us.'

Isaiah Isaiah was a prophet* in Judah. He spoke for God to the kings of Judah. He spoke of the Messiah. Jesus read from the scroll of Isaiah in the synagogue when he began his public ministry.

Israel The land where the Jewish people lived. The people of Israel is another name for the Jewish people. They are the children of Abraham, Isaac, and Jacob.

Israelites The people of Israel.

Jairus Jairus was a Jewish leader. He asked Jesus to help his daughter who was sick. The girl died before Jesus reached her. But she came back to life when Jesus spoke to her.

James James was a disciple of Jesus. He was the brother of John the disciple. Jesus took James, along with Peter and John, with him on the mount where they saw Jesus' glory when Jesus spoke with Moses and Elijah.

Jericho A city; the Israelites* destroyed it when they came into the land that God had promised them (Joshua 6).

Jerusalem Jerusalem was the city where David lived. Solomon built the Temple* there. It was the chief city of Judah.

Jew/Jewish A Jew is a person that is born from Abraham, Isaac and Jacob, and their children. A person that has the faith* of the Jews.

John John was an Apostle*. He was a very close friend of Jesus as well. He listened carefully to Jesus and wrote many of the things he said in his book. When he was an old man, God gave him a dream*. He wrote what he saw in the last book of the Bible.

John the Baptist John the Baptist was the man who went before Jesus to prepare the way. He called people to turn from their sin*. He baptized* Jesus.

Jordan River The Jordan River was part of the border of Israel* on the east. The people crossed this river to get into the land God promised to Abraham. Later, Jesus was baptized in this river.

Joseph Joseph was a man who had promised to take Mary as his wife. When he learned that Mary was to have a baby, he decided not to marry her. When an angel came to tell him that the child was to be the Messiah and that God had given Mary the child, he married her and cared for Jesus as his child.

Joseph of Arimathea A rich man from the town of Arimathea*. He was a follower* of Jesus. Joseph cared for Jesus' body after he died.

Judas Iscariot A disciple of Jesus. He was one of the first twelve men that Jesus chose as his followers. Judas is the one who betrayed Jesus in the Garden of Gethsemane.* He kissed Jesus as a sign to show the soldiers who they should arrest.

Jude One of Jesus' disciples.

Judea Judea was one of the areas that was in the southern part of Israel in Jesus' day. The Dead Sea was on Judea's eastern border. The cities of Jerusalem and Bethlehem were part of Judea.

Kingdom A kingdom is where a king rules; a land where a king rules.

Kingdom of heaven The kingdom of heaven is where God rules. Jesus is King of Kings and will someday rule on earth as he does in heaven.

Lamb of God Jesus is called the Lamb of God. This shows that Jesus was the sacrifice* that was offered for us. He did this so that God could forgive* the bad things we do.

Law Rules that a ruler makes to tell people how to live. The rules God gave Moses for the people of Israel.

Lazarus Lazarus was a friend of Jesus. Jesus sometimes stayed at his home. He became sick and died. Jesus raised him from the dead.

Levites Levites was the name given to the sons of Levi. They were the priests* for God's people. They helped the people worship* God. They took care of the Temple.*

Lord Lord is the name for God in the Bible. It means that he is above all other things and ruler of all things. A name that we use for Jesus when we obey him.

Luke Luke was a man who followed Jesus. He was not an Apostle*. But he knew many of these men and heard their stories. He sometimes went with Paul on his trips. His book about Jesus is in the Bible. It is one of the gospels*.

Mark Mark was a young man when he began to follow Jesus. He spent time with Peter. He told the story of Jesus in the book that bears his name.

Martha Martha was a friend and follower of Jesus. She was the sister of Mary and Lazarus.

Mary Mary was the mother of Jesus. She cared for him as a boy. She was there when he died on the cross*. Remember: There are many different women named Mary in the New Testament*.

Mary (sister of Martha and Lazarus) Mary was a friend and follower of Jesus. She was the sister of Martha and Lazarus.

Mary Magdalene Mary Magdalene was a woman who was healed by Jesus. He cast seven evil spirits* from her. She then followed Jesus and was there when Jesus was put on the cross. She went to the tomb of Jesus and was one of the first people to see him after he rose from the grave.

Matthew Matthew collected taxes before he met Jesus. Jesus called him to leave his job and follow him. Matthew was an Apostle*.

Messiah Messiah is a title for the special servant of God. It means 'the one God chose to anoint.'* Samuel* put oil on David* to show that God had chosen him to be king. So the Jews* used the name Messiah to refer to the king that God promised to send from David's family. This king would rescue the people from all of their enemies. He was the king who would build God's kingdom.* That kingdom would last for ever. When Jesus* came, he said that he was the Messiah that the Jews had waited for. He was the Christ.* Christ is the Greek word for Messiah. But many of the Jews did not believe* him.

Micah Micah was a prophet* who spoke to Israel for God 600 years before Jesus was born. It was Micah who said that the Messiah would be born in Bethlehem.

Miracle wonderful works that God does by his power; a wonderful thing that shows that a person's message is from God.

Mount of Olives A place in the Garden of Gethsemane where Jesus went to pray after his last meal with his disciples. Jesus was arrested here after Judas gave him to his enemies.

Moses Moses was born in Egypt when Jacob's family lived there. God chose Moses to help the Jews. He rescued them and brought them out of Egypt.

Most High A name for God.

Myrrh A precious oil; the wise men gave myrrh to the baby Jesus as a gift.

Nazareth Nazareth was the place where Jesus had lived until he began his public ministry. Joseph settled his family in Nazareth after they returned from Egypt where he had fled to protect Jesus from Herod.

New Testament The last part of the the Bible,* which the writers wrote after Jesus* rose up from the dead. It is about the things that Jesus did and taught. It is also about the church.*

Nicodemus Nicodemus was a ruler of the Jews*. He came to Jesus to ask him some important questions. He was there when Jesus died. He helped to bury his body.

Offering A gift for God (or false gods) from the priest and people; an animal to be offered as a sacrifice*.

Old Testament The first part of the Bible;* the holy* books that men wrote before Jesus* was born.

Parable a story, like those told by Jesus, to explain the things that he taught; a saying or a story from which you can understand two things or where something is hidden.

Passover an important holy* day for the Jews*. They ate a special meal on this day every year. This was to remember that God freed them from being slaves in Egypt at the time of Moses.

Paul/Saul Paul was a man who did not believe* in Jesus. His name was Saul then. Jesus came to him and made him an Apostle.* That is when Jesus changed his name to Paul. He wrote many letters. Some of those letters are now in the Bible.*

Peace When we do not fight God or other people; when we have no troubles in our mind or spirit;* when we are friendly to other people.

Pearl A little white ball of hard material that shines. It is very valuable. A small, soft animal that lives inside a shell makes pearls. This animal lives in the sea.

Perea An area east of the Jordan River. Jesus taught there with his disciples.

Peter/Simon Peter Peter was an Apostle*. He was one of the first people to see Jesus after he came back from death. God used him to help the church* get started.

Pharisees a group of Jews* who thought that they kept all God's rules. They did not like the things that Jesus taught. They thought that they did not do any wrong things. So, they thought that they were very important and clever.

Philip One of Jesus' disciples.

Pilate The governor of Judea when Jesus went to Jerusalem for the last time. He was the one who organized the trial of Jesus. Pilate was the one who ordered that Jesus be sent to die on a cross.

Praise To say how good a person is; to tell God how great he is, as when we are praying and singing to him.

Preach To tell and explain the good news about Jesus Christ to someone or a group of people.

Priest The priests in Israel* were the men who helped people worship* God. The priests began to do this work when Moses* was the leader. They took care of God's Tent. They made the sacrifices* for the people. When Solomon built the Temple*, they took care of it. They served the people up until the time that Jesus lived and for many years after. There were also priests in other nations. They sacrificed to false gods.

Prophet those who were able to tell other people what God wanted; people who spoke for God a long time ago; someone who told of things that would happen in the future; a person who spoke the words that God gave them to speak.

Repent To turn from sin* to do what God wants us to do; to decide not to do the bad things you did before; when you turn your mind away from bad things.

Resurrection To be raised from death, to come alive again after you have died.

Romans Romans were the people who lived in the city of Rome. Or people who were part of the nation ruled from Rome.

Rome Rome was the most famous city in the world at the time of Jesus. Their soldiers fought and defeated many countries. They made the people obey the rules of Rome. They made them pay taxes to Rome. The people could not rule themselves, but they had to obey the laws of Rome.

Sabbath A day of rest in which the people are not allowed to work. In the Old Testament* it was Saturday (from sunset on Friday to sunset on Saturday); day seven of the week for the Jews*. It is a special day for the Jews*, for doing what is pleasing to God.

Sacrifice To kill an animal as an offering to God so that God will forgive* an evil* thing. The Israelites were told to make sacrifices to God. Usually, it was a special animal that the priests killed and burned on the altar*. Some people made sacrifices to false gods. Something a person gives up for a special purpose can also be called a sacrifice; giving up something that is important to you on behalf of someone (God); offering yourself to work for God; Christ's death for us.

Samaria Samaria was a city in Israel*. It was the capital of the northern kingdom*. It was also the name given to the area or territory around that city. It was where the Samaritans lived.

Samaritan Samaritans were the people that lived in Samaria. They were part Jews*, but they did not worship* the same way that the Jews* did. The Jews* did not like the Samaritans.

Sanhedrin The leaders of the priests*, the important Jews* and the teachers of the Law* meeting together. The most important priest led them. There were 71 men in the Sanhedrin. Together, they judged people. The people in the Sanhedrin had great power.

Satan Satan is another name for Devil.* Satan is the worst of the bad angels. He works against God and God's people.

Save to rescue someone from danger; when God rescues a person from the result and power of sin*; to save a person from the bad results of the bad things in their lives. Jesus is called the savior - the one who saves us; the one who rescues; someone who will bring us back to God from the bad things we have done; someone who saves us from the bad things other people have done to us.

Savior Jesus Christ is the savior. Someone who brings us back to God and rescues us from being punished for the bad things we have done.

Scripture The writings of God's holy* words; another name for the Bible*; the book which tells God's truth and shows that the Jesus is Lord*, the savior* and Messiah*.

Scroll A long piece of paper or animal's skin. It is fixed around two poles of wood. It usually has writing on it.

Sea of Galilee The sea of Galilee was the body of water that formed part of the border of Galilee. It was sometimes called the Lake of Galilee. It is the main water source for the Jordan River. Jesus grew up near this lake and did many miracles there when he began his ministry.

Shepherd A person who cares for a group of sheep. The Bible* sometimes says that God is like a shepherd. He cares for his people. Jesus said that he was the good shepherd. He would give his life for his people (sheep).

Siloam pool A location where Jesus performed a miracle.* He placed mud on a blind man's eyes, then told him to wash in the Siloam pool. When the man did this, he could see.

Simeon Simeon at the Temple is the "just and devout" man of Jerusalem who, according to Luke 2:25–35, met Mary, Joseph, and Jesus as they entered the Temple to fulfill the requirements of the Law of Moses on the 40th day from Jesus' birth, i. e. the presentation of Jesus at the Temple. According to the Biblical account, the Holy Spirit visited Simeon and revealed to him that he would not die until he had seen the Christ of God.

Simon As Jesus was going to be killed on a cross*, Simon was made by one of the soldiers to carry Jesus' cross for him. Simon was from Cyrene, a city in Northern Africa.

Simon the Zealot One of Jesus' disciples.

Sin/sinned/sinful When people do things against God or other people; when we do not obey the commands of God; when we do not do what God wants us to do; the evil that is in us which we have from birth.

Sinner A sinner is a person who does not obey God and does sinful things.

Son of God One of the titles Jesus used to speak of himself. He wanted people to know that he had come from God, that God was his Father. This was another way to tell people that he was the Messiah.

Son of Man One of the titles Jesus used to speak of himself. The title came from the book of Daniel in the Old Testament. It spoke of the servant God would send to rescue his people and do work that only God could do. The title was one that spoke of Jesus as the Messiah.

Spirit A being that does not have a body and no one can see it. God is spirit. God made other spirit beings (angels*) that we cannot see who can be good or bad. The spirit of a person is sometimes called the person's soul.

Synagogue A synagogue is a Jewish building where Jewish people went for worship. On the Sabbath, local Jews would meet for prayer and Scripture reading. On one occasion, Jesus read from the prophet* Isaiah during a gathering in the synagogue.

Temple The Temple was the place Solomon built for God. It was the place for Israel* to worship* God. It was the place where people made sacrifices*. It was the place where God could be with his people. The temple was in the city of Jerusalem.

Thomas Thomas was an Apostle*. He was there when Jesus died. But he was not there the first time people saw Jesus after he rose from death. So Thomas doubted. But, when he did see Jesus, he believed.

Transfiguration A change in appearance; the change in Jesus' face and looks when he was on a high mountain with three of his disciples.*

Triumphal entry The story of Jesus arriving in Jerusalem a few days before he was killed on a cross.

Trust to follow something or someone you think is true; to believe in someone or something; to have faith* and act in faith*; to believe in someone you think speaks the truth.

Virgin someone who has never been with another person to have sex. Jesus' mother Mary was a virgin when God came to her. She had never been with a man.

Worship The way we should act when we are with God. We honor him with prayer. We sing and speak praise* to him. We bend down before him to honor him. Worship is a way that we show that God is great and we love him. To show honor to God; to act in ways that please God. Some people do not worship God. They worship false gods.

Yeast People put yeast into flour and water to make bread. The yeast grows in the bread and it causes the bread to rise.

Zacchaeus Zacchaeus was a tax collector in the City of Jericho.* Jesus spoke to Zacchaeus and visited his home. Zacchaeus had been a sinful man who was changed by Jesus' kindness to him.

Zechariah Zechariah was a priest in Jerusalem during the time of Jesus' birth. He was married to Elizabeth. They could have no children. The angel Gabriel met Zechariah as he served in the Temple. He announced that Zechariah and Elizabeth would have a son. Zechariah would become the father of John the Baptist.

Zion Jerusalem,* the City of God.

APPENDIX

Below is a list of all events in the earthly life of Jesus. This is not a complete list of every text in the Gospels. Some people who read the Gospels do not always make the list exactly the same. But the list gives a general timeline of events in Jesus' life. We hope it will help you to understand the life and ministry of Jesus.

There are many more stories on this list than the ones that we included in this book. But, when you see a line that **looks like this one (bold print)**, that story is part of the sixty (60) stories in this book.

JESUS' BIRTH, CHILDHOOD, AND EARLY YEARS[1]
Matthew 1: Luke 1

1. **John the Baptist*'s birth is promised** – Luke 1:5-25
2. **Jesus' birth is promised** – Luke 1:26-38
3. Mary* visits cousin Elizabeth* – Luke 1:39-56
4. **The birth and naming of John the Baptist*** – Luke 1:57-66
5. Zechariah*'s song at John*'s birth – Luke 1:67-80
6. **Joseph*'s dream* and obedience** – Matthew 1:18-24
7. **The birth of Jesus** – Matthew 1:25a, Luke 2:1-7
8. **Angels* announce Jesus' birth to shepherds*** – Luke 2:8-20
9. **Circumcision* and naming of Jesus** – Matthew 1:25, Luke 2:21
10. **Jesus is presented in the temple*** – Luke 2:22-38
11. **The wise men visit and honor* Jesus as a child** – Matthew 2:1-12
12. **Joseph* and Mary* escape to Egypt* with Jesus** – Matthew 2:13-15
13. **Herod* has children killed** – Matthew 2:16-18
14. **Jesus' family returns to Nazareth*** – Matthew 2:19-23, Luke 2:39-40
15. **Jesus in the temple* at age 12** – Luke 2:41-52

JESUS BEGINS TO TEACH THE PEOPLE[2]
Matthew 3:13; Mark 1:9;Luke 3:21-23

16. **John the Baptist* preaches* and baptizes*** – Matthew 3:1-12, Mark 1:1-8, Luke 3:1-18
17. **Jesus' baptism*** – Matthew 3:13-17, Mark 1:9-11, Luke 3:21-23
18. **Jesus is tempted** – Matthew 4:1-11, Mark 1:12-13, Luke 4:1-13
19. **John the Baptist* calls Jesus the Messiah*** – John 1:19-34

---

1   This early period of Jesus' life would last until he was about 30 years old (Luke 3:23).

2   This early period of Jesus' teaching would last about 6 months.

JESUS TEACHES IN GALILEE*³
Matthew 4:12; Mark 6:1; Luke 4:16

---

3   Jesus went from place to place in Galilee for 12 to 18 months.

45. Jesus criticized for picking grain on the Sabbath* – Matthew 12:1-8, Mark 2:23-28, Luke 6:1-5
46. Jesus heals a hand on the Sabbath* – Matthew 12:9-14, Mark 3:1-6, Luke 6:6-11
47. Jesus heals at the Sea of Galilee* – Matthew 12:15-21, Mark 3:7-12
48. **Jesus chooses the twelve disciples*** – Matthew 10:2-4, Mark 3:13-19, Luke 6:12-16
49. **Jesus preaches* the "Sermon on the Mount"** – Matthew 5:1–7:29, Luke 6:17-49
50. **Jesus heals a Roman* officer's servant** – Matthew 8:5-13, Luke 7:1-10
51. Jesus brings a widow's son back to life – Luke 7:11-17
52. Jesus reassures John the Baptist* – Matthew 11:1-19, Luke 7:18-35
53. The people of Galilee* do not repent* – Matthew 11:20-24
54. Jesus invites the tired to follow him, promises rest – Matthew 11:25-30
55. **Jesus is blessed* by a sinful* woman** – Luke 7:36-50
56. Jesus travels through Galilee* again – Luke 8:1-3
57. Jesus heals a blind man – Matthew 12:22-24
58. Jesus is accused by teachers of the law – Matthew 12:25-37, Mark 3:20-30
59. Jesus criticizes people who rely on signs instead of faith* – Matthew 12:38-45
60. Jesus' mother and brothers do not understand him – Matthew 12:46-50, Mark 3:31-35, Luke 8:19-21
61. **Jesus teaches The Parable* of the Farmer** – Matthew 13:1-9, Mark 4:1-9, Luke 8:4-8
62. Jesus explains to his disciples why he teaches in parables* – Matthew 13:10-17, Mark 4:10-12, Luke 8:10
63. **Jesus explains The Parable of the Sower** – Matthew 13:18-23, Mark 4:13-20, Luke 8:9-15
64. Jesus tells a story about a lamp – Mark 4:21-25, Luke 8:16-18
65. Jesus tells the story of the growing seed – Mark 4:26-29
66. Jesus teaches The Parable* of the the Weeds – Matthew 13:24-30
67. Jesus teaches The Parable* of the Mustard Seed – Matthew 13:31-32, Mark 4:30-32, Luke 13:18-19
68. Jesus teaches The Parable* of the Yeast* – Matthew 13:33, Luke 13:20-21
69. Jesus satisfies Psalm 78:2 – Matthew 13:34-35, Mark 4:33-34
70. Jesus explains The Parable* of the Weeds – Matthew 13:36-43
71. **Jesus teaches The Parable* of the Hidden Treasure** – Matthew 13:44
72. Jesus teaches The Parable* of the Pearl* – Matthew 13:45-46
73. Jesus teaches The Parable* of the Net – Matthew 13:47-50
74. Jesus teaches The Parable* of the Land Owner – Matthew 13:51-52
75. **Jesus calms the storm** – Matthew 8:18,23-27, Mark 4:35-41, Luke 8:22-25
76. **Jesus heals a mad man** – Matthew 8:28-34, Mark 5:1-20, Luke 8:26-39

77. Jesus heals a bleeding woman – Matthew 9:20-22, Mark 5:24b-34, Luke 8:42b-48
78. **Jesus heals Jairus*' daughter** – Matthew 9:18-19,23-26, Mark 5:21-24a,35-43, Luke 8:40-42a,49-56
79. Jesus heals two blind men – Matthew 9:27-31
80. Jesus heals a man controlled by an evil spirit* – Matthew 9:32-34
81. Jesus is rejected in Nazareth* again – Matthew 13:53-58, Mark 6:1-6a
82. Jesus sends out his disciples* to preach* and heal – Matthew 10:1,5-42, Mark 6:6b-13, Luke 9:1-6
83. **Herod* orders John the Baptist* to be killed** – Matthew 14:6-12, Mark 6:17-29
84. Herod* wonders if John the Baptist* came back to life as Jesus – Mark 6:14-16, Luke 9:7-9

JESUS LEAVES GALILEE*4
Matthew 14:13; Luke 9:10

85. **Jesus feeds five thousand people** – Matthew 14:13-21, Mark 6:30-44, Luke 9:10-17, John 6:1-15
86. **Jesus walks on water** – Matthew 14:22-33, Mark 6:45-52, Luke 6:16-21
87. Jesus offers food that lasts for ever – John 6:22-71
88. Jesus and the Pharisees* disagree about what makes someone unclean – Matthew 15:1-20, Mark 7:1-23
89. Jesus heals a girl who is controlled by an evil spirit* – Matthew 15:21-28, Mark 7:24-30
90. Jesus heals a deaf man – Mark 7:31-37
91. Jesus heals many people on a mountain near Sea of Galilee* – Matthew 15:29-31
92. Jesus feeds four thousand people – Matthew 15:32-38, Mark 8:1-10
93. Teachers of the law* ask for a sign – Matthew 15:39-16:4, Mark 8:11-12
94. Jesus warns others about the influence of the teachers of the law* – Matthew 16:5-12, Mark 8:13-21
95. Jesus heals a blind man – Mark 8:22-26
96. Peter* says that Jesus is the Christ* – Matthew 16:13-20, Mark 8:27-30, Luke 9:18-20
97. Jesus tells of his coming death and resurrection* – Matthew 16:21-28, Mark 8:31-9:1, Luke 9:21-27
98. **Jesus' appearance changes before the disciples*** – Matthew 17:1-8, Mark 9:2-8, Luke 9:28-36
99. **Jesus talks about Elijah* and John the Baptist*** – Matthew 17:9-13, Mark 9:9-13

---

4   Jesus may have gone outside of Galilee for about 6 months

100. Jesus sends an evil spirit** out of a boy – Matthew 17:14-21, Mark 9:14-29, Luke 9:37-43a
101. Jesus speaks again about his coming death and resurrection* – Matthew 17:22-23, Mark 9:30-32, Luke 9:43b-45
102. Jesus produces a coin to pay the Temple* Tax – Matthew 17:24-27
103. Jesus teaches about service and gives warnings – Matthew 18:1-11, Mark 9:33-50, Luke 9:46-50
104. Jesus teaches about acting in his name – Matthew 18:15-20
105. **Jesus teaches The Parable* of the Servant Who Had No Mercy** – Matthew 18:21-35
106. Jesus refuses to destroy a Samaritan* village – Luke 9:51-56
107. Jesus tells people what they must give up to follow him – Matthew 8:19-22, Luke 9:57-62

JESUS TEACHES IN JUDEA*5
John 7:10; Luke 9:51

108. Jesus hesitates to go to Jerusalem* – John 7:1-9
109. Jesus speaks at a feast– John 7:10-52
110. Jesus forgives* a sinful* woman – John 7:53-8:11
111. Jesus says he is the light of the world – John 8:12-59
112. **Jesus heals a man who was born blind** – John 9:1-41
113. Jesus calls himself the Good Shepherd* – John 10:1-21
114. Jesus sends out 70 men to teach others – Luke 10:1-24
115. **Jesus teaches The Parable* of the Good Samaritan*** – Luke 10:25-37
116. **Jesus visits Mary* and Martha* in Bethany*** – Luke 10:38-42
117. Jesus teaches the disciples* how to pray – Matthew 6:9-15, Luke 11:1-13
118. The people accuse Jesus of healing through an evil spirit* – Luke 11:14-26
119. Jesus responds to a woman in the crowd – Luke 11:27-28
120. Jesus says that the Son of Man* is a sign from God – Luke 11:29-36
121. Teachers of the law* criticize Jesus – Luke 11:37-54
122. Jesus warns the people not to trust* the Pharisees*– Luke 12:1-12
123. **Jesus teaches The Parable* of the Rich Fool** – Luke 12:13-21
124. Jesus teaches The Parables* of the Wild Flowers and the Ravens – Luke 12:22-34
125. Jesus talks about his future return to earth – Luke 12:35-48
126. Jesus talks about his coming death – Luke 12:49-59
127. Jesus teaches The Parable* of the Fig Tree – Luke 13:1-9
128. Jesus heals a woman with a crooked back – Luke 13:10-17
129. Jesus says that he is God's Son – John 10:22-42

---

5 Jesus went to Jerusalem for the Feast of Tabernacles and may have stayed in Judea about 3 months.

JESUS TEACHES IN PEREA*[6]
John 10:40-42

130. Jesus teaches about the Narrow Way – Luke 13:22-30
131. Jesus is warned about Herod* – Luke 13:31-33
132. Jesus is sad for Jerusalem* – Matthew 23:37-39, Luke 13:34-35
133. Jesus heals a sick man – Luke 14:1-6
134. Jesus teaches about being humble – Luke 14:7-14
135. Jesus teaches The Parable* of the Large Feast – Luke 14:15-24
136. The cost of following Jesus – Luke 14:25-35
137. **Jesus teaches The Parable* of the Lost Sheep** – Matthew 18:12-14, Luke 15:1-7
138. **Jesus teaches The Parable* of the Lost Coin** – Luke 15:8-10
139. **Jesus teaches The Parable* of the Lost Son** – Luke 15:11-32
140. Jesus teaches The Parable* of the Clever Manager – Luke 16:1-18
141. Jesus teaches The Parable* of the Rich Man and Lazarus* – Luke 16:19-31
142. Jesus teaches about faith* and service – Luke 17:1-10
143. **Jesus brings Lazarus* back to life** – John 11:1-44
144. The Jewish* leaders plan against Jesus – John 11:45-54
145. **Jesus heals 10 sick men on his way to Jerusalem*** – Luke 17:11-19
146. Jesus teaches about the coming of God's kingdom* – Luke 17:20-37
147. The Parable* of the Widow Who Would Not Give Up – Luke 18:1-8
148. **The story of the Pharisee* and the tax collector** – Luke 18:9-14
149. Jesus speaks about divorce and marrying again – Matthew 19:1-12, Mark 10:1-12, Luke 16:18
150. **Jesus welcomes little children** – Matthew 19:13-15, Mark 10:13-16, Luke 18:15-17
151. Jesus and the rich, young ruler – Matthew 19:16-30, Mark 10:17-31, Luke 18:18-30
152. **Jesus teaches The Parable* of Workers and Wages** – Matthew 20:1-16
153. Jesus again speaks about his death and resurrection* – Matthew 20:17-19, Mark 10:32-34, Luke 18:31-34
154. James* and John* ask Jesus for a favor – Matthew 20:20-28, Mark 10:35-45
155. **Jesus heals Blind Bartimaeus*** – Matthew 20:29-34, Mark 10:46-52, Luke 18:35-43
156. **Jesus talks with Zacchaeus*** – Luke 19:1-10
157. Jesus teaches the story of three servants – Luke 19:11-27

---

6   Jesus may have spent 3 months on the "other side of the Jordan" known as Perea.

JESUS TRAVELS TO JERUSALEM* AND DIES ON A CROSS*[7]
Matthew 21:1-9; Mark 11:1-10; Luke 19:28-38

158. The Jewish* leaders plan against Jesus and Lazarus* – John 11:55-12:1, 9-11
159. Mary* of Bethany* blesses* Jesus – Matthew 26:6-13, Mark 14:3-9, John 12:2-8
160. **Jesus comes to Jerusalem* as Lord***– Matthew 21:1-11, Mark 11:1-11, Luke 19:28-44, John 12:12-19
161. Jesus makes a fig tree dry up – Matthew 21:18-19, Mark 11:12-14
162. **Jesus cleanses the temple* and teaches there** – Matthew 21:12-17, Mark 11:15-19, Luke 19:45-48
163. People from Greece ask to see Jesus – John 12:20-22
164. Jesus speaks about his coming death – John 12:23-36
165. Jews* continue not to believe* in Jesus – John 12:37-50
166. Jesus teaches about a dried up fig tree – Matthew 21:20-22, Mark 11:20-26
167. The Jewish* leaders question Jesus' authority – Matthew 21:23-27, Mark 11:27-33, Luke 20:1-8
168. Jesus teaches The Parable* of Two Sons – Matthew 21:28-32
169. Jesus teaches The Parable of the Land Owner – Matthew 21:33-46, Mark 12:1-12, Luke 20:9-19
170. Jesus teaches The Parable* of the Wedding Feast – Matthew 22:1-14
171. Jesus is asked about paying tax to Caesar* – Matthew 22:15-22, Mark 12:13-17, Luke 20:20-26
172. Teachers of the law* ask Jesus about resurrection* – Matthew 22:23-33, Mark 12:18-27, Luke 20:27-40
173. Jesus teaches The Greatest Command – Matthew 22:34-40, Mark 12:28-34
174. Jesus speaks about the family line of the Messiah – Matthew 22:41-46, Mark 12:35-37, Luke 20:41-44
175. Jesus warns against doing things for the wrong reasons – Matthew 23:1-36, Mark 12:38-40, Luke 20:45-47
176. **Jesus teaches about the widow's small coin** – Mark 12:41-44, Luke 21:1-4
177. Jesus speaks about the future – Matthew 24:1-51, Mark 13:1-37, Luke 21:5-38
178. **Jesus teaches The Parable* of the Ten Virgins*** – Matthew 25:1-13
179. **Jesus teaches The Parable* of the Three Servants** – Matthew 25:14-30
180. Jesus uses the example of sheep and goats – Matthew 25:31-46
181. The Jewish* leaders continue to plan against Jesus – Matthew 26:1-5, Mark 14:1-2, Luke 22:1-2
182. Judas* plans to betray Jesus – Matthew 26:14-16, Mark 14:10-11, Luke 22:3-6
183. **The disciples* prepare for the Passover* meal** – Matthew 26:17-19, Mark 14:12-16, Luke 22:7-13

---

7   These stories took place during the final week of Jesus' life before he was raised from death.

184. **Jesus washes the disciples*' feet** – John 13:1-20
185. **Jesus says Judas* will betray him** – Matthew 26:20-25, Mark 14:17-21, Luke 22:21-23, John 13:21-30
186. Jesus gives a new command – John 13:31-35
187. **Jesus says his disciples* will deny him** – Matthew 26:31-35, Mark 14:27-31, Luke 22:31-38, John 13:36-38
188. Jesus teaches about true power – Luke 22:24-30
189. **Jesus and his disciples* have the Last Supper** – Matthew 26:26-30, Mark 14:22-25, Luke 22:14-20
190. Jesus says goodbye to his disciples* – John 14:1-16:33
191. Jesus prays for his disciples* – John 17:1-26
192. **Jesus' pain in the Garden of Gethsemane*** – Matthew 26:36-46, Mark 14:26,32-42, Luke 22:39-46
193. **Jesus is betrayed and arrested** – Matthew 26:47-56, Mark 14:43-52, Luke 22:47-53, John 18:1-12
194. Jesus is brought before Annas – John 18:12-14,19-23
195. Jesus is brought before Caiaphas* – Matthew 26:57,59-68, Mark 14:53-65, Luke 22:54,63-65, John 18:24
196. **Peter* denies knowing Jesus** – Matthew 26:58,69-75, Mark 14:54,66-72, Luke 22:54-62, John 18:15-18,25-27
197. The Sanhedrin* find Jesus guilty – Matthew 27:1-2, Mark 15:1a, Luke 22:66-71
198. Judas Iscariot* kills himself – Matthew 27:3-10
199. **Jesus' trial before Pilate*** – Matthew 27:2,11-14, Mark 15:1b-5, Luke 23:1-5, John 18:28-38
200. Pilate sends Jesus to Herod Antipas – Luke 23:6-10
201. **Herod returns Jesus to Pilate*** – Luke 23:11-12
202. **Jesus will be put to death in place of Barabbas*** – Matthew 27:15-26, Mark 15:6-15, Luke 23:13-25, John 18:39-19:16
203. **Soldiers make fun of Jesus** – Matthew 27:27-31, Mark 15:16-20
204. **Simon* carries Jesus' cross*** – Matthew 27:32, Mark 15:21, Luke 23:26
205. **Jesus speaks to the women who followed him** – Luke 23:27-31
206. **Jesus is killed on a cross*** – Matthew 27:33-37, Mark 15:22-26, Luke 23:33-34, John 19:17-24
207. **The women who followed Jesus watch his death on the cross*** – Matthew 27:55-56, Mark 15:40-41, Luke 23:49, John 19:25-27
208. **The crowd makes fun of Jesus** – Matthew 27:39-43, Mark 15:29-32, Luke 23:35-38
209. **Two robbers are killed on crosses* with Jesus** – Matthew 27:38,44, Mark 15:27-28, Luke 23:32,39-43
210. **Amazing events happen at Jesus' death** – Matthew 27:45-54, Mark 15:33-39, Luke 23:44-48, John 19:28-30

211. **Soldiers put a spear in Jesus' side** – John 19:31-37
212. **Jesus is buried in the grave of Joseph of Arimathea*** – Matthew 27:57-60, Mark 15:42-46, Luke 23:50-54, John 19:38-42
213. Women mourn at Jesus' grave – Matthew 27:61, Mark 15:47, Luke 23:55-56

RESURRECTION* AND APPEARANCES[8]
Matthew 28:1-4; Luke 24:1-2

214. **Jesus comes alive again** – Matthew 28:2-4
215. **Women visit the grave to anoint* Jesus' body** – Matthew 28:1, Mark 16:1-4, Luke 24:1-2
216. **Women find the empty grave** – Matthew 28:5-7, Mark 16:5-8, Luke 24:3-8, John 20:1-2
217. **Peter and John hurry to the grave** – Luke 24:9-12, John 20:3-10
218. **Jesus appears to Mary Magdalene*** – Mark 16:9-11, John 20:11-18
219. **Jesus sends the women to tell the disciples*** – Matthew 28:8-10
220. The Jewish* leaders bribe soldiers – Matthew 28:11-15
221. **Jesus comes to two men on the road to Emmaus*** – Luke 24:13-35
222. Many other people see Jesus – Mark 16:12-13
223. **Jesus appears to his disciples* while Thomas* is away**– Luke 24:36-49, John 20:19-25
224. **Jesus appears to Thomas* and the other disciples*** – John 20:26-29
225. The disciples* catch many fish at the Sea of Galilee* – John 21:1-14
226. Jesus gives Peter* an important job – John 21:15-19
227. Jesus and Peter talk about Apostle* John*'s future – John 21:20-24
228. **Jesus tells the disciples* to continue his work** – Matthew 28:16-20, Mark 16:14-18, Acts 1:4-8
229. **Jesus goes up into heaven*, to be with God, the Father** – Mark 16:19-20, Luke 24:50-53, Acts 1:9

---

8   The forty days before Jesus went up into the heavens.

Acknowledgements

This book is full of stories about Jesus. We wrote them to be clear and simple to read. But writing a book like this is not so simple. Now that the book is finished, we want to thank the many people who helped us write it.

One of the first tasks we had was to put all of these stories in the correct order. Several people have written books that helped us do that. Some are still writing books about how the gospel stories fit together. Some of the writers are no longer living. Thank you to John Broadus, A.T. Robertson, Lorraine Boettner, Robert Thomas, William Gundry, Harold Hoehner, Kurt Aland, George W. Knight, John H. Kerr, Edgar Goodspeed, Ernest De Witt Burton, Burton Throckmorten, Jr., Orville Daniel, and the editors of the Zondervan NIV Study Bible.

Thank you to John and Kim Walton. Together, they wrote The Bible Story Handbook. The advice they share in that book helped to shape the way we tell the stories in this book.

Thank you also to our friends at StoryRunners (www.storyrunners.org). They spent time with us, teaching us the best way to write and tell stories from the Bible.

Thank you to John Walsh and his colleagues at BibleTelling (bibletelling.org) for encouraging us in this project. He has faithfully coached and modeled Bible story-telling for decades.

Thank you to the people at Simply the Story (www.simplythestory.org) and Discovery Bible Study (www.dbsguide.org). Both helped us craft both the stories and the discussion guide for this book.

Special thanks to the people who helped us put this set of stories together. Audrey Carroll Christenson helped work on the first drafts of the stories in the spring of 2020. Leah Seier and Susan Moore helped to edit the structure and content of the many versions of the stories that followed. Scottie Garber-Roberts put the book in final form by editing and managing the project to the way it reads today. The book looks the way it does because of Jason Chittum of One32 Design (www.one32design.com). He is the one whose design work makes Clear and Simple Media books appear so clean and attractive.